CHARLE
COM

Other books by Michael and
Mollie Hardwick include:

The Sherlock Holmes Companion
The Man who was Sherlock Holmes
Sherlock Holmes Investigates
Four Sherlock Holmes Plays
(published by John Murray)

Stories from Dickens
(published by Edward Arnold)

Writers' Houses: a literary journey in England
(published by Phoenix House)

Alfred Deller: a Singularity of Voice
(published by Cassell)

THE
CHARLES DICKENS
COMPANION

Michael and Mollie Hardwick

JOHN MURRAY
Fifty Albemarle Street London

Printed in Great Britain by
Latimer Trend & Co. Ltd., Whitstable, Kent

7195 1873 3

FOREWORD

This book is intended both as a reference work for Dickensians and as an introduction for all who are on the threshold of that wonderful world which Dickens created and peopled with characters who have passed into the gallery of immortals. Quilp, Mrs. Gamp, Dick Swiveller, Traddles, Lord Frederick Verisopht, Micawber and a host of others are no longer oddities or grotesques, but real people, for we have met them all. To discover Dickens in youth is to make a friend for life: a friend who matures as the reader matures and who is for ever revealing new depths of meaning and humanity as the reader's own comprehension of life widens and expands.

We have planned our book in sections. Summaries of the plots will enable the new reader to choose those books which most appeal to him in setting and subject, remembering always that it is the flesh which Dickens puts on these bare bones that gives them their life. He was not, in Francis Mears' words, 'our best plotter.'

Quotations are chosen to illustrate typically Dickensian subjects and to convey something of Dickens's highly individual flavour, as well as the immense variety of wit, wisdom and outlook of his unforgettable characters. The essays and sketches collected in *Miscellaneous Papers*, *The Uncommercial Traveller* and *Sketches by Boz* are not itemized but have been used as sources of quotation.

In a Who's Who of the significant characters from the major works, it is obviously not possible to include more than a selection from a total of over fifteen hundred. Characters from the minor works have reluctantly been omitted: for instance, those of the five Christmas Books and of the long short story *No Thoroughfare* are listed, but those of the shorter Christmas Stories are not. The world of Dickens is a very wide one with a tremendous cosmography. We have sadly had to exclude many passages that are full of delight but so woven into their context that they cannot be separated without spoiling them.

Any selection from Dickens must inevitably be a personal one, but we gratefully acknowledge the assistance of Mr. John Greaves, Hon. Secretary of the Dickens Fellowship, who has scrutinized our text for errors and made some characteristically helpful suggestions.

Illustrations have been selected mainly from the 'classic' illustrators of Dickens's works—George Cruikshank, 'Phiz' (Hablot K. Browne), John Leech, Richard Doyle, George Cattermole and Daniel Maclise, but Luke Fildes and Fred Walker are also represented.

We would have liked to give more space to Charles Dickens's amazing personal qualities, which constantly tantalize the biographer but which can help us to understand the universality of his books. The adjectives used about him by those who knew him are significant: 'great—generous—inimitable—jovial—noble—magical—compelling—kindly', words which constantly recur in their descriptions. Among all the characters Dickens created, none is more remarkable than Charles Dickens himself: the man who could cheerfully lampoon a friend, as he lampooned Leigh Hunt in the character of Harold Skimpole, and yet who had a genius for friendship: the dissatisfied husband and unwilling parent, who became the god of British domesticity; the chronicler of the joys of hearth and home, who was in private life broad-minded far beyond his contemporaries, the advocate of easier divorce, brighter Sundays, funerals without pomp, and the abolition of capital punishment; the man who rejoiced in the contemplation and description of food and drink, and yet was himself abstemious to a degree.

That he attacked the evils of his day in his books is well known, but his personal work for reform is not so often acknowledged. He dared to speak against slavery in the America of 1842; in his own country he helped to found the Hospital for Sick Children in Great Ormond Street, and his ideals lay behind the Education Act that was passed in the year of his death. In his journals *Household Words* and *All the Year Round* he worked constantly for social reforms, and even his public readings were directed at bringing the classes together. 'In this world a great deal of the bitterness among us arises from an imperfect understanding of one another.'

To seek in his works for graphic portrayals of the iniquities of his time is to seek in vain. Deference to public prudery restrained him from doing with his pen what Hogarth had done with pencil and brush in the previous century. For example, Dickens worked hard for the welfare of women driven to prostitution, but could not bring himself to deal realistically with such a subject in his stories. Nancy, in *Oliver Twist*, is a feebly-drawn, over-refined and wholly unconvincing example of her real-life counterparts in Victorian London. The prissiness of the worldly, experienced Dickens contrasts interestingly with the passionate strength of the Brontë sisters, writing in their cloistered isolation. Their handicap was ignorance: his was sentimental theatricality.

In fact, had Charles Dickens not been a great author, he might have been a great actor, a great preacher or a great politician. The adjective remains constant. As it is, the world may be thankful that his genius created a permanent record, and that he wrote at a time when the pen was most influential.

MICHAEL AND MOLLIE HARDWICK

CONTENTS

CHRONOLOGY OF
CHARLES DICKENS'S WORKS

1833   A DINNER IN POPLAR WALK (afterwards in SKETCHES BY BOZ called MR. MINNS AND HIS COUSIN): *The Monthly Magazine*.

1834–5   SKETCHES BY BOZ, printed as SKETCHES OF LONDON and SCENES AND CHARACTERS: *The Monthly Magazine, Morning Chronicle* and *Evening Chronicle* and *Bell's Life in London*.

1836   Collected SKETCHES BY BOZ in two volumes: published by John Macrone.

1836   Second series of SKETCHES BY BOZ in one volume: published by John Macrone.

1836–7   THE POSTHUMOUS PAPERS OF THE PICKWICK CLUB: in monthly numbers published by Chapman & Hall.

1837   First number of the journal *Bentley's Miscellany*: edited by Charles Dickens.

1837–8   OLIVER TWIST: *Bentley's Miscellany*. Published in three volumes by Richard Bentley in 1838.

1838–9   LIFE AND ADVENTURES OF NICHOLAS NICKLEBY: In monthly numbers published by Chapman & Hall. Issued complete in October, 1839.

1839   SKETCHES BY BOZ, first complete edition: published by Chapman & Hall.

WHO'S WHO

ADAMS. Head boy at Dr. Strong's school. 'He looked like a young clergyman in his white cravat, but he was very affable and good-humoured.'—*David Copperfield*.

ADAMS, CAPTAIN. Lord Frederick Verisopht's second at the duel with Sir Mulberry Hawk. 'The two seconds . . . both utterly heartless: both men about town; both thoroughly initiated in its worst vices . . . they were naturally gentlemen of unblemished honour themselves; and of great nicety concerning the honour of other people.' —*Nicholas Nickleby*.

ADAMS, JACK. An acquaintance of Lord Feenix. 'Jack—little Jack—man with a cast in his eye and slight impediment in his speech. Man who sat for somebody's borough.' —*Dombey and Son*.

AFFERY. Maid to Mrs. Clennam. (Portrait, p. 41.) The wife of Jeremiah Flintwinch. 'Lived in terror of her husband and Mrs. Clennam, the clever ones.'—*Little Dorrit*.

AGED, THE. Mr. Wemmick's old father. 'A very old man in a flannel coat: clean, cheerful, comfortable, and well cared for, but intensely deaf.'—*Great Expectations*.

AKERSHEM, SOPHRONIA. Married to Mr. Alfred Lammle under the impression that he was a man of property. 'Mature young lady; raven locks; and complexion that lights up well when well powdered—as it is.' —*Our Mutual Friend*.

Arabella Allen

ALLEN, ARABELLA. Sister of Ben Allen. 'A black-eyed young lady, in a very nice little pair of boots, with fur round the top.'—*The Pickwick Papers*.

ALLEN, BENJAMIN. Medical student and friend of Bob Sawyer. 'A coarse, stout, thick-set young man, with black hair cut rather short, and a white face cut rather long; he was embellished with spectacles, and wore a white neckerchief. He presented altogether rather a mildewy appearance, and emitted a fragrant odour of full-flavoured Cubas.'—*The Pickwick Papers*.

ALICE. The youngest of the Five Sisters of York, in 'The Inside Passenger's Tale'. 'A fair creature of sixteen . . . the blushing tints in the soft bloom on the fruit, or the delicate painting on the flower, are not more exquisite than was the blending of the rose and lily in her gentle face.'—*Nicholas Nickleby*.

ALPHONSE. Page to Mrs. Wititterly. 'A little page; so little indeed, that his body would not hold, in ordinary array, the number of small buttons which are indispensable to a page's costume, and they were consequently obliged to be stuck on four abreast; but, if ever an Alphonse carried plain Bill in his face and figure, that page was the boy.' —*Nicholas Nickleby*.

AMELIA. A housemaid at Dr. Blimber's School who befriended Paul Dombey. 'A pretty young woman in leather gloves, cleaning a stove.'—*Dombey and Son*.

ANALYTICAL CHEMIST, THE. The Veneerings' butler, a gloomy character. 'Always seeming to say, after "Chablis, sir?—you wouldn't if you knew what it's made of".'—*Our Mutual Friend*.

AUNT, MR. F's. An aunt of Mr. Finching. 'An amazing little old woman, with a face like a staring wooden doll, too cheap for expression, and a stiff yellow wig, perched unevenly on the top of her head, as if the child

Mr. F's aunt

who owned the doll had driven a tack through it anywhere,
so that it only got fastened on.'—*Little Dorrit.*

AVENGER, THE. Otherwise Pepper, Pip's boy. 'For,
after I had made this monster (out of the refuse of my
washerwoman's family) and had clothed him with a blue
coat, canary waistcoat, white cravat, creamy breeches, and
the boots . . . I had to find him a little to do and a great deal
to eat; and with both of these horrible requirements he
haunted my existence.'—*Great Expectations.*

BABLEY, RICHARD. *See* DICK, MR.—*David Copperfield.*

BACHELOR, THE. A friend of the clergyman of the parish
of which Mr. Marton was schoolmaster. 'The little old
gentleman was the active spirit of the place; the adjuster of
all differences; the promoter of all merry-makings; the
dispenser of his friends' bounty, and of no small charity of
his own besides; the universal mediator, comforter, and
friend.'—*The Old Curiosity Shop.*

BADGER, BAYHAM. A doctor with whom Richard Carstone studied medicine. 'A pink, fresh-faced, crisp-looking
gentleman, with a weak voice, white teeth, light hair, and
surprised eyes.'—*Bleak House.*

BADGER, MRS. BAYHAM. Previously
married to (1) Captain Swosser of the Royal
Navy; (2) Professor Dingo. 'A lady of
about fifty . . . youthfully dressed, and of
a very fine complexion. She was surrounded in the drawing room by various
objects indicative of her painting a little,
playing the piano a little, playing the guitar a
little, playing the harp a little, singing a little,
working a little, reading a little, writing

Mrs.
Bayham
Badger

poetry a little, and botanising a little; if I add to the little list of her accomplishments that she rouged a little, I do not mean that there was any harm in it.'—*Bleak House*.

BAGMAN, THE. Jovial character and teller of tales encountered by Pickwickians at The Peacock Inn, Eatans-will. 'A stout hale personage of about forty, with only one eye—a very bright black eye, which twinkled with a roguish expression of fun and good humour.'—*Pickwick Papers*.

BAGNET, MATTHEW. A friend of George Rouncewell. 'An ex-artillery-man, tall and upright, with shaggy eye-brows, and whiskers like the fibres of a coconut, not a hair upon his head, and a torrid complexion.'—*Bleak House*.

BAGNET, MRS. MATTHEW. 'Not at all an ill-looking woman; rather large-boned, a little coarse in the grain, and freckled by the sun and wind, which have tanned her hair upon the forehead; but healthy, wholesome and bright-eyed . . . the old girl, says Mr Bagnet . . . is a thoroughly fine woman.'—*Bleak House*.

BAGNET, QUEBEC AND MALTA. Daughters of Mr. and Mrs. Bagnet. 'These young ladies—not supposed to have been actually christened by the names applied to them, though always so called in the family, from the places of their birth in barracks . . .'—*Bleak House*.

BAGNET, WOOLWICH. Son of Mr. and Mrs. Bagnet. 'The type and model of a young drummer.'—*Bleak House*.

BAGSTOCK, MAJOR. A retired army officer, acquaintance of Mr. Dombey. Self-styled 'old Bagstock,' 'old Joey

Bagstock,' 'Joey B.' and similar names.  'A wooden-featured, blue-faced Major, with his eyes staring out of his head . . . it may be doubted whether there ever was a more entirely selfish person at heart—or at stomach is perhaps a better expression, seeing that he was more decidedly endowed with that latter organ than with the former.' —*Dombey and Son.*

*Major
Bagstock*

BAILEY, CAPTAIN. David Copperfield's rival at the Larkins' Ball. 'I do waltz (pretty well, too, as it happens) and I take Miss Larkins out. I take her sternly from the side of Captain Bailey. He is wretched no doubt, but he is nothing to me.'—*David Copperfield.*

BAILEY, JUNIOR. Page at Mrs. Todgers' boarding house. Later 'tiger' or groom to Tigg Montague. 'If any piece of crockery, a dish or otherwise, chanced to slip through his hands, he let it go with perfect good breeding, and never added to the painful emotions of the company by exhibiting the least regret; nor did he, by hurrying to and fro, disturb the repose of the assembly, as many well-trained servants do.'—*Martin Chuzzlewit.*

BAMBER, JACK. One of the law clerks whom Mr. Pickwick met at the Magpie and Stump. Also mentioned in *Master Humphrey's Clock.* 'A little, yellow, high-shouldered man; there was a fixed grim smile perpetually on his countenance; he leant his chin on a long skinny hand, with nails of extraordinary length; and, as he inclined his head to one side, and looked keenly out from beneath his ragged grey eyebrows, there was a strange wild slyness in his leer, quite repulsive to behold.'—*Pickwick Papers.*

BANGHAM, MRS. Charwoman and messenger in the

Marshalsea Prison, attendant at Little Dorrit's birth. 'Who was not a prisoner (though she had been once) but was the popular medium of communication with the outer world.'—*Little Dorrit.*

BANTAM, MR. ANGELO CYRUS. Master of Ceremonies at the Pump Room, Bath. 'A charming young man, of not much more than fifty; dressed in a very bright blue coat, with resplendent buttons, black trousers, and the thinnest possible pair of highly polished boots . . . his features were contracted into a perpetual smile; and his teeth were in such perfect order that it was difficult at a small distance to tell the real from the false.'—*Pickwick Papers.*

Mr. Angelo Cyrus Bantam

BAPS, MR. A dancing-master in charge of the breaking-up party at Dr. Blimber's. 'A very grave gentleman, with a slow and measured manner of speaking.'—*Dombey and Son.*

BARBARA. Servant-girl at Mr. Garland's, and later wife of Kit. 'There was such a kitchen as was never before seen or heard of out of a toy shop window; with everything in it as bright and glowing, and as precisely ordered, as Barbara herself.'—*The Old Curiosity Shop.*

BARBARA'S MOTHER. '. . . came in with astonishing accounts of the fineness of the weather out of doors, but with a very large umbrella notwithstanding; for people like Barbara's mother seldom make holiday without one.' —*The Old Curiosity Shop.*

BARBARY, MISS. Aunt and godmother of Esther Summerson, and sister to Lady Dedlock. 'She was a good, good woman; she went to Church three times every Sunday, and to morning prayers on Wednesdays and Fridays, and to lectures whenever there were lectures; she was handsome, and if she had ever smiled would have been (I used to think) like an angel; but she never smiled; she was always grave and strict.'—*Bleak House*.

BARDELL, MR., deceased. 'After enjoying for many years the esteem and confidence of his Sovereign, as one of the Guardians of his royal revenues, glided almost imperceptibly from the world, to seek elsewhere for that repose and peace which a custom-house can never afford.'—*Pickwick Papers*.

BARDELL, MRS. Mr. Pickwick's landlady. (Portrait, p. 114.) 'The relict and sole executrix of a deceased custom-house officer—was a comely woman, of bustling manners, and agreeable appearance; with a natural genius for cooking, improved by study and long practice into an exquisite talent.'—*Pickwick Papers*.

BARDELL, TOMMY. Son of Mrs. Bardell. 'Clad in a tight suit of corduroy spangled with brass buttons of considerable size.'—*Pickwick Papers*.

BARKIS. The Yarmouth carrier, and future husband of Clara Peggotty. He proposed to her by sending the cryptic message—'Barkis is willin'.' 'The carrier had a way of keeping his head down, like his horse, and of drooping sleepily forward as he drove, with one of his arms on each of his knees. I say drove, but it struck me that the cart would have gone to Yarmouth quite as well without him, for the horse did all that; and as to conversation, he had no idea of it but whistling.'—*David Copperfield*.

BARLEY, BILL. Father of Clara. 'Old Gruffandgrim.'
—*Great Expectations*.

BARLEY, CLARA. Future wife of Herbert Pocket. 'A very
pretty, slight, dark-eyed girl of twenty or so . . . there was
something so natural and winning in Clara's resigned way
. . . and something so confiding, loving, and innocent, in
her modest manner of yielding herself to Herbert's
embracing arm.'—*Great Expectations*.

BARNACLES, THE. 'A very high family, and a very large
family. They were dispersed all over the Public Offices,
and held all sorts of public places. Either the nation was
under a load of obligation to the Barnacles; or the
Barnacles were under a load of obligation to the nation; it
was not quite unanimously settled which.'—*Little Dorrit*.

BARNACLE, LORD DECIMUS. '. . . with the very smell of
Despatch Boxes upon him.' 'In the great art of How not
to do it, Lord Decimus had long sustained the highest
glory of the Barnacle family.'—*Little Dorrit*.

BARNACLE, CLARENCE (Barnacle Junior). Son of Tite
Barnacle. 'Had a youthful aspect, and the fluffiest little
whisker, perhaps that ever was seen.'—*Little Dorrit*.

BARNACLE, FERDINAND. Private Secretary to Lord
Decimus Barnacle. 'This dashing young Barnacle, in a
word, was likely to become a statesman, and to make a
figure.'—*Little Dorrit*.

BARNACLE, MR. TITE. Of the Circumlocution Office. 'A
buttoned-up man, and consequently a weighty one. All
buttoned-up men are weighty. All buttoned-up men are
believed in . . . Mr. Tite Barnacle never would have
passed for half his current value, unless his coat had been
always buttoned-up to his white cravat.'—*Little Dorrit*.

BARNACLE, MRS. TITE. 'The expensive Mrs. Tite Barnacle, *née* Stiltstalking, who made the Quarter Days so long in coming.'—*Little Dorrit.*

BARNEY. Waiter at the Three Cripples public-house. 'Younger than Fagin but nearly as vile and repulsive in appearance.'—*Oliver Twist.*

BARRONNEAU, MADAME. Young widow of Henri Barroneau, whom Rigaud married and was later charged with murdering. 'She was two-and-twenty; she had gained a reputation for beauty, and (which is often another thing) was beautiful.'—*Little Dorrit.*

BARSAD, JOHN. Alias of Solomon Pross. French spy in the pay of England, afterwards a turnkey in the Conciergerie. 'Age, about forty years; height, about five feet nine; black hair; complexion dark; generally, rather handsome visage; eyes dark, face long, thin and sallow; nose aquiline but not straight, having a peculiar inclination towards the left cheek; expression, therefore, sinister.'—*A Tale of Two Cities.*

BATES, CHARLEY. One of Fagin's gang of thieves. 'Charley Bates exhibited some very loose notions concerning the rights of property.'—*Oliver Twist.*

BAZZARD, MR. Clerk to Mr. Grewgious. 'A pale, puffy-faced, dark-haired person of thirty, with big dark eyes that wholly wanted lustre, and a dissatisfied, doughy complexion that seemed to ask to be sent to the baker's.' —*Edwin Drood.*

BEADLE, HARRIET. *See* TATTYCORAM—*Little Dorrit.*

BEDWIN, MRS. Housekeeper to Mr. Brownlow. 'A motherly old lady very neatly and precisely dressed.' —*Oliver Twist*.

BELLE. Scrooge's boyhood sweetheart. 'A fair young girl in a mourning-dress, in whose eyes there were tears, which sparkled in the light that shone out of the Ghost of Christmas Past.'—*A Christmas Carol*.

BELVAWNEY, MISS. Actress in Mr. Crummles' company. 'Seldom aspired to speaking parts, and usually went on as a page, in white silk hose, to stand with one leg bent and contemplate the audience.'—*Nicholas Nickleby*.

BERINTHIA ('Berry') 'Mrs. Pipchin's middle-aged niece, her good-natured and devoted slave, but possessing a gaunt and iron-bound aspect, and much afflicted with boils on her nose.'—*Dombey and Son*.

BET. Prostitute and companion of Nancy. 'They wore a good deal of hair, not very neatly turned up behind, and were rather untidy about the shoes and stockings.'—*Oliver Twist*.

BETSEY. The slipshod maid of Mrs. Raddle, 'who might have passed for the neglected daughter of a superannuated dustman in very reduced circumstances.'—*The Pickwick Papers*.

BEVAN, MR. A kindly American, from Massachusetts, who befriends Martin Chuzzlewit and lends him money to return to England. 'There was a cordial candour in his manner, and an engaging confidence that it would not be abused.'—*Martin Chuzzlewit*.

BIDDY. Granddaughter of Mr. Wopsle's great-aunt, and later Joe Gargery's second wife. 'Her hair always wanted

brushing, her hands always wanted washing, and her shoes always wanted mending and pulling up at the heel.'
—*Great Expectations*.

BILLICKIN, MRS. Rosa Bud's landlady. 'Personal faintness, and an overpowering personal candour, were the distinguishing features of Mrs. Billickin's organization.'
—*Edwin Drood*.

BITHERSTONE, MASTER. A boarder at Mrs. Pipchin's. 'Paul had enough to do . . . watching all the workings of his countenance, with the interest attaching to a boy of mysterious and terrible experiences.'—*Dombey and Son*.

BITZER. Model boy at Mr. Gradgrind's; later worked at Bounderby's Bank. 'He held the respectable office of general spy and informer in the establishment.'—*Hard Times*.

BLACKPOOL, STEPHEN. Factory hand in Bounderby's Mills. 'A rather stooping man with a knitted brow.'—*Hard Times*.

Stephen Blackpool

BLACKPOOL, MRS. STEPHEN. 'Such a woman—a disabled, drunken creature, barely able to preserve her sitting posture by steadying herself with one begrimed hand on the floor.'—*Hard Times*.

BLANDOIS. *See* RIGAUD—*Little Dorrit*.

BLATHERS. A Bow Street Officer. 'A stout personage, of middle height, aged about fifty, with shiny black hair cropped pretty close, half whiskers, a round face and sharp eyes.'—*Oliver Twist*.

BLIGHT, YOUNG. Mortimer Lightwood's office-boy. 'The managing clerk, junior clerk, common law clerk, conveyancing clerk, chancery clerk, every refinement and department of clerk . . .'—*Our Mutual Friend.*

BLIMBER, DOCTOR. Principal of boys' school at Brighton. 'A portly gentleman, in a suit of black . . . he had a bald head, highly polished, a deep voice, and a chin so very double that it was a wonder how he ever managed to shave into the creases.' —*Dombey and Son.*

Dr. Blimber

BLIMBER, MRS. 'She said at evening parties that if she could have known Cicero she thought she could have died contented.'—*Dombey and Son.*

BLIMBER, MISS CORNELIA. Their daughter, later wife of Mr. Feeder, B.A. 'There was no light nonsense about Miss Blimber. She kept her hair short and crisp, and wore spectacles. She was dry and sandy, with working in the graves of deceased languages.'—*Dombey and Son.*

BLOCKITT, MRS. Nurse who attended Mrs. Dombey. 'A simpering piece of faded gentility.'—*Dombey and Son.*

BLOTTON, MR. Of Aldgate. Member of the Pickwick Club, who called Mr. Pickwick a humbug. 'He repelled the hon. gent.'s false and scurrilous accusation, with profound contempt.'—*The Pickwick Papers.*

BOFFIN, NICODEMUS (Noddy). Heir to the elder Mr. Harmon, and originally his servant. 'A broad, round-

shouldered, one-sided old fellow
. . . Both as to his dress and to
himself he was of an overlapping
rhinoceros build.'—*Our Mutual
Friend*.

BOFFIN, MRS. NICODEMUS. 'A
stout lady of a rubicund and cheerful aspect . . . a smiling creature,
broad of figure and simple of
nature.'—*Our Mutual Friend*.

BOLDER, MASTER. Pupil at
Dotheboys Hall. 'An unhealthy-
looking boy, with warts all over
his hands.'—*Nicholas Nickleby*.

Nicodemus Boffin

BOLDWIG, CAPTAIN. Neighbour of Sir Geoffrey Man-
ning. 'A little fierce man, in a stiff black neckerchief.'
—*The Pickwick Papers*.

BOLO, MISS. Mr. Pickwick's whist partner at Bath. 'Of an
ancient and whist-like appearance.'—*The Pickwick Papers*.

BOLTER, MORRIS. *See* CLAYPOLE—*Oliver Twist*.

BOODLE, LORD. Guest at Chesney Wold. 'Of considerable reputation with his party, who has known what office
is.'—*Bleak House*.

BOUNDERBY, JOSIAH. A self-made man, later husband of
Louisa Gradgrind. 'A big man with a stare and a metallic
laugh; a man made out of a coarse material.'—*Hard
Times*.

BOWLEY, SIR JOSEPH. A philanthropist, self-styled 'the poor man's friend'. 'Another, and an older, and a much statelier gentleman . . . looked complacently from time to time at his own picture.'—*The Chimes*.

BOXER. John Peerybingle's dog. 'Everybody knew him all along the road, especially the fowls and pigs . . . with his body all on one side, and his ears pricked up inquisitively, and that knob of a tail making the most of itself in the air.' —*The Cricket on the Hearth*.

BOYTHORN, LAWRENCE. Friend of John Jarndyce. 'Then the most impetuous boy in the world, and he is now the most impetuous man . . . he is a tremendous fellow.' —*Bleak House*.

BRASS, SALLY. Sister to Sampson Brass. 'A kind of Amazon at common law . . . of a gaunt and bony figure, and a resolute bearing.' —*The Old Curiosity Shop*.

BRASS, SAMPSON. Quilp's solicitor. 'A tall, meagre man, with a nose like a wen . . . he had a cringing manner, but a very harsh voice, and his blandest smiles were so extremely forbidding . . .'—*The Old Curiosity Shop*.

BRAVASSA, MISS. Actress in Mr. Crummles' company. 'The beautiful Miss Bravassa,

Sally Brass

who had once had her likeness taken in character by an engraver's apprentice.'—*Nicholas Nickleby*.

BRAY, MADELINE. Later wife of Nicholas Nickleby. (Portrait, p. 68.) 'Of a very slight and delicate figure, but exquisitely shaped . . . a countenance of most uncommon beauty, though shaded by a cloud of sadness.'—*Nicholas Nickleby*.

BRAY, WALTER. Father of Madeline. 'His features presented the remains of a handsome countenance, but one in which the embers of strong and impetuous passions were . . . to be traced.'—*Nicholas Nickleby*.

BRICK, MR. JEFFERSON. War correspondent to *The New York Rowdy Journal*. 'A small young gentleman, of very juvenile appearance, and unwholesomely pale in the face; partly perhaps from intense thought, but partly, there is no doubt, from the excessive chewing of tobacco.'—*Martin Chuzzlewit*.

BRITAIN, BENJAMIN ('Little Britain'). Servant to Dr. Jeddler, later landlord of the Nutmeg Grater, and husband of Clemency Newcome. 'You see, I've made a good many investigations of one sort and another in my time, having always been of an inquiring turn of mind.'—*The Battle of Life*.

BRITTLES. Mrs. Maylie's servant. 'A lad of all work, who, having entered her service a mere child, was treated as a promising young boy still, though he was something past thirty.'—*Oliver Twist*.

BROGLEY, MR. Broker. Friend of Sol Gills, who took possession of The Wooden Midshipman. 'A moist-eyed, pink-complexioned, crisp-haired man, of a bulky figure and an easy temper.'—*Dombey and Son*.

Brooker. Returned convict, once clerk to Ralph Nickleby. 'A spare, dark, withered man . . . with a stooping body and a very sinister face . . . having about him an indefinable manner of depression and degradation.'—*Nicholas Nickleby*.

Browdie, John. A Yorkshire corn factor, fiancé of Matilda Price. 'Something over six feet high, with a face and body rather above the due proportion than below it.' —*Nicholas Nickleby*.

Brown, Mrs. Self-styled 'Good Mrs. Brown', mother of Alice Marwood, and abductor of Florence Dombey. 'A very ugly old woman, with red rims round her eyes and a mouth which mumbled and chattered of itself when she was not speaking.' —*Dombey and Son*.

'Good Mrs. Brown'

Brownlow, Mr. Friend to Oliver Twist. (Portrait, p. 67.) 'A very respectable-looking personage, with a powdered head and gold spectacles.'—*Oliver Twist*.

Bucket, Inspector. A detective officer. 'A stoutly-built, steady-looking, sharp-eyed man . . . thoughtful Mr. Bucket is, as a man with weighty work to do, but composed, sure, confident.'—*Bleak House*.

Bucket, Mrs. 'A lady of a natural detective genius . . . which has paused at the level of a clever amateur.'—*Bleak House*.

BUD, ROSA. Pupil at the Nuns' House Ladies' Seminary; engaged to Edwin Drood. 'Wonderfully pretty, wonderfully childish, wonderfully whimsical.'—*Edwin Drood*.

Rosa Bud

BUFFY, MR., M.P. A guest at Chesney Wold. 'Contends across the table with someone else that the shipwreck of the country . . . is attributable to Cuffy.'—*Bleak House*.

BULL'S-EYE. Bill Sikes's dog. (Portrait p. 83.) 'A white shaggy dog, with his face scratched and torn in twenty different places.'—*Oliver Twist*.

BUMBLE, MR. The parish beadle. (Portrait p. 29.) 'Mr. Bumble was a fat man and a choleric.' 'He was in the full bloom and pride of beadlehood; his cocked hat and coat were dazzling in the morning sun; and he clutched his cane with the vigorous tenacity of health and power.' —*Oliver Twist*.

BUNSBY, JACK. Captain of the *Cautious Clara*, friend of Captain Cuttle, and later husband of Mrs. MacStinger. 'Another bulkhead—human and very large—with one stationary eye in the mahogany face, and one revolving one, on the principle of some light-houses.'—*Dombey and Son*.

BUZFUZ, Serjeant. Counsel for Mrs. Bardell in Bardell *v.* Pickwick. 'Who's that red-faced man who said it was a fine morning?'—*The Pickwick Papers*.

CAMILLA, MRS. Sister of Matthew Pocket, met by Pip at Miss Havisham's. 'I began to think it was a mercy she had any features at all, so very blank and high was the dead wall of her face.'—*Great Expectations*.

CARKER, HARRIET. Sister of the brothers James and John Carker. 'This slight, small, patient figure, neatly dressed in homely stuffs . . . is she, his sister, who of all the world went over to him in his shame, and put her hand in his.'—*Dombey and Son*.

CARKER, JAMES. Manager for Dombey and Son. 'Of a florid complexion, and with two unbroken rows of glistening teeth, whose regularity and whiteness were quite distressing.'—*Dombey and Son*.

CARKER, JOHN. Junior clerk in Dombey and Son's counting-house. 'He was not old,

James Carker

but his hair was white . . . the fire of his eyes, the expression of his features, the very voice in which he spoke, were all subdued and quenched, as if the spirit within him lay in ashes.'—*Dombey and Son*.

CARSTONE, RICHARD. Ward in Chancery, later husband of Ada Clare. 'A handsome youth, with an ingenuous face, and a most engaging laugh.' —*Bleak House*.

Richard Carstone

CARTON, SYDNEY. Barrister, and double of Charles Darnay. '. . . of good abilities and good emotions, incapable of their directed exercise, incapable of his own help, and his own happiness, sensible of the blight on him, and resigning himself to let it eat him away.'—*A Tale of Two Cities.*

Sydney Carton

CASBY, MR. CHRISTOPHER. Rack-renting proprietor of slum property, and father of Flora. '. . . so grey, so slow, so quiet, so impassionate, so very bumpy in the head, Patriarch was the word for him.'—*Little Dorrit.*

CAVALETTO, JOHN BAPTIST. Italian refugee employed by Arthur Clennam. 'A sunburnt, quick, lithe, little man . . . earrings in his brown ears; white teeth lighting up his grotesque brown face.'—*Little Dorrit.*

CHADBAND, MR. A lay preacher. 'A large yellow man, with a fat smile, and a general appearance of having a good deal of train oil in his system.'—*Bleak House.*

CHADBAND, MRS. Originally Mrs. Rachael, Esther Summerson's nurse. 'A stern, severe-looking, silent woman.'—*Bleak House.*

Mr. Chadband

CHARLOTTE. Servant to Mrs. Sowerberry, who ran away with Noah Claypole. 'A slatternly girl, shoes down at heel,

and blue worsted stockings very much out of repair.'
—*Oliver Twist*.

CHEERYBLE, CHARLES. One of the twin brothers
Cheeryble. 'A sturdy old fellow . . . with such a pleasant
smile playing about his mouth, and such a comical
expression of mingled slyness, simplicity, kindheartedness
and good humour.'—*Nicholas Nickleby*.

CHEERYBLE, EDWIN. The other twin. 'Another old
gentleman, the very type and model of himself, the face of
each lighted up by beaming looks of affection.'—*Nicholas
Nickleby*.

CHEERYBLE, FRANK. Nephew of the Brothers Cheeryble,
and later husband of Kate Nickleby. 'A sprightly, good-
humoured, pleasant fellow, with much both in his countenance and disposition that reminded Nicholas very strongly
of the kind-hearted brothers.'—*Nicholas Nickleby*.

CHEGGS, MR. Rival of Dick Swiveller. 'Mr. Cheggs was
a market-gardener, and shy in the presence of ladies.'—*The
Old Curiosity Shop*.

CHESTER, EDWARD. Son
of Sir John Chester, and
later husband of Emma
Haredale. 'Travel-stained
though he was, he was well
and richly attired, and
without being over-dressed
looked a gallant gentle-
man.'—*Barnaby Rudge*.

Sir John Chester

CHESTER, SIR JOHN.
Man of the world, enemy

of the Haredales. 'A staid, grave, placid gentleman . . . soft spoken, delicately made, precise and elegant.'—*Barnaby Rudge*.

CHESTLE, MR. A hop grower, successful suitor of the eldest Miss Larkins. 'A plain elderly gentleman.' —*David Copperfield*.

CHICK, MR. JOHN. 'A stout, bald gentleman, with a very large face, and his hands continually in his pockets, and who had a tendency in his nature to whistle and hum tunes.'—*Dombey and Son*.

CHICK, MRS. LOUISA. Sister of Mr. Dombey. 'With a kind of screw in her face and carriage expressive of suppressed emotion.'—*Dombey and Son*.

CHICKENSTALKER, MRS. (MRS. TUGBY). 'Fat company, rosy-cheeked company, comfortable company.' 'Always inclined to corpulency, even in the days when he had known her as established in the general line.'—*The Chimes*.

CHILDERS, MR. E. W. B. One of Sleary's circus troupe. 'A most remarkable sort of Centaur, compounded of the stable and the playhouse.'—*Hard Times*.

CHILLIP, DOCTOR. Attendant at David Copperfield's birth. 'He was the meekest of his sex, the mildest of little men. He carried his head on one side, partly in modest depreciation of himself, partly in modest propitiation of everybody else.'—*David Copperfield*.

CHITLING, TOM. One of Fagin's gang. 'He had small twinkling eyes, and a pockmarked face, wore a fur cap, a dark corduroy jacket, greasy fustian trousers and an apron.'—*Oliver Twist*.

CHIVERY, JOHN. Turnkey at the Marshalsea Prison. 'There was native delicacy in Mr. Chivery—true politeness; though his exterior had very much of a turnkey about it, and not the least of a gentleman.' —*Little Dorrit.*

CHIVERY, JOHN. Son of the turnkey. 'Young John was gentle likewise; but he was great of soul; poetical, expansive, faithful.' —*Little Dorrit.*

John Chivery Jnr.

CHIVERY, MRS. John's mother. 'A comfortable-looking woman, much respected about Horsemonger Lane for her feelings and her conversation.'—*Little Dorrit.*

CHOKE, GENERAL CYRUS. Member of the Eden Land Corporation. 'A very lank gentleman, in a loose limp white cravat, a long white waistcoat, and a black greatcoat.' —*Martin Chuzzlewit.*

CHOLLOP, HANNIBAL. American visitor to Eden. 'A lean person, in a blue frock and straw hat, with a short black pipe in his mouth.'—*Martin Chuzzlewit.*

CHRISTMAS PAST, THE GHOST OF. Scrooge's first guide. 'It was a strange figure—like a child; yet not so like a child as an old man, viewed through some supernatural medium which gave him the appearance of having receded from the view, and being diminished to a child's proportions.'—*A Christmas Carol.*

CHRISTMAS PRESENT, THE GHOST OF. Scrooge's second guide. 'Its dark brown curls were long and free; free as its genial face, its sparkling eye, its open hand, its cheery voice, its unconstrained demeanour, and its joyful air.'—*A Christmas Carol.*

CHRISTMAS YET TO COME, THE GHOST OF. Scrooge's third guide. 'It was shrouded in a deep black garment, which concealed its head, its face, its form, and left nothing of it visible save one outstretched hand.'—*A Christmas Carol.*

CHUCKSTER, MR. Clerk to the notary, Mr. Witherden. '. . . settling his neck more gracefully in his stock; and secretly arranging his whiskers, by the aid of a little triangular bit of looking glass.'—*The Old Curiosity Shop.*

CHUFFEY. Clerk to Anthony Chuzzlewit and Son. 'A little, blear-eyed, weazen faced, ancient man . . . he looked as if he had been put away and forgotten half a century before, and somebody had just found him in the lumber closet.'—*Martin Chuzzlewit.*

CHUZZLEWIT, ANTHONY. Brother of old Martin. 'The face of the old man so sharpened by the wariness and cunning of his life, that it seemed to cut him a passage through the crowded room.'—*Martin Chuzzlewit.*

CHUZZLEWIT, JONAS. Son of Anthony. 'The education of Mr. Jonas had been conducted from his cradle on the strictest principles of the main chance.'—*Martin Chuzzlewit.*

Jonas Chuzzlewit

CHUZZLEWIT, MARTIN, the elder, grandfather of young Martin. 'I have no pleasure in hoarding. I have no pleasure in the possession of money ... pain and bitterness are the only goods it ever could procure for me.'—*Martin Chuzzlewit*.

CHUZZLEWIT, MARTIN, the younger. 'He was young—one-and-twenty perhaps —and handsome, with a keen dark eye, and a quickness of look and manner.'— *Martin Chuzzlewit*.

CICERO. Negro truckman in New York, encountered by Martin Chuzzlewit and Mark Tapley. 'Bought his freedom, which he got pretty cheap at last, on account of his strength being nearly gone, and he being ill.'—*Martin Chuzzlewit*.

Old Martin
Chuzzlewit

CLARE, ADA. Ward in Chancery; later wife of Richard Carstone. 'A beautiful girl, with such rich golden hair, such soft blue eyes, and such a bright, innocent, trusting face.'—*Bleak House*.

CLARRIKER. Partner to Herbert Pocket. 'A worthy young merchant or shipping broker, not long established in business.'—*Great Expectations*.

CLAYPOLE, NOAH, alias Morris Bolter. Assistant to Mr. Sowerberry and later a thief. 'A large-headed small-eyed youth of lumbering make and heavy countenance.'—*Oliver Twist*.

CLEAVER, FANNY ('JENNY WREN'). A crippled doll's dressmaker. 'She would glance at the visitors out of the corners of her grey eyes, with a look that out-sharpened all her other sharpness. She had an elfin chin, that was capable of great expression.'—*Our Mutual Friend.*

Fanny Cleaver

CLEAVER, MR. Jenny Wren's drunken father, known as 'Mr. Dolls'. 'The whole indecorous threadbare ruin, from the broken shoes to the prematurely grey scanty hair, grovelled . . . '—*Our Mutual Friend.*

CLENNAM, ARTHUR. Adopted son of Mrs. Clennam, later married to Little Dorrit. 'I am the only child of parents who weighed, measured, and priced everything.'—*Little Dorrit.*

Arthur Clennam

CLENNAM, MRS. Adoptive mother of Arthur. (Portrait p. 146.) 'Stern of face and unrelenting of heart, she would sit all day behind a Bible—bound, like her own construction of it, in the hardest, barest, and straitest boards.'—*Little Dorrit.*

CLERGYMAN, THE. Of the parish where Mr. Marton was school-master. 'A simple-hearted old gentleman, of a shrinking subdued spirit, accustomed to retirement, and very little acquainted with the world.'—*The Old Curiosity Shop.*

CLERGYMAN, THE. Guest at Dingley Dell, singer of 'The Ivy Green', and teller of 'The Convict's Return.'—*The Pickwick Papers.*

CLICKETT (THE ORFLING). Mrs. Micawber's maid of-all-work. 'A dark-complexioned young woman, with a habit of snorting.'—*David Copperfield*.

CLUPPINS, MRS. Friend of Mrs. Bardell and sister of Mrs. Raddle. 'A little brisk busy-looking woman.'—*The Pickwick Papers*.

CLY, ROGER. Ex-servant of Darnay, later a spy. 'The virtuous servant Roger Cly.'—*A Tale of Two Cities*.

COBB, TOM. General chandler and Post Office keeper at Chigwell. 'Beyond all question the dullest dog of the party.'—*Barnaby Rudge*.

CODGER, MISS. American literary lady. 'Sticking on her forehead, by invisible means, was a massive cameo, in size and shape like the raspberry tart which is ordinarily sold for a penny.'—*Martin Chuzzlewit*.

CODLIN, THOMAS. Joint proprietor with Short of a Punch and Judy show. 'God bless you; recollect the friend; Codlin's the friend, not Short; Short's all very well, as far as he goes, but the real friend is Codlin—not Short.'—*The Old Curiosity Shop*.

COILER, MRS. A neighbour of the Pockets. 'She had a serpentine way of coming close at me . . . which was altogether snaky and fork-tongued.'—*Great Expectations*.

COMPEYSON. A criminal, partner of Magwitch. 'He'd no more heart than an iron file, he was as cold as death, and he had the head of the Devil.'—*Great Expectations*.

COPPERFIELD, DAVID. 'Whether I shall
turn out to be the hero of my own life or
whether that station will be held by anybody
else these pages must show.'—*David Copperfield*.

David
Copperfield

COPPERFIELD, MRS. Mother of David.
Married Mr. Murdstone *en secondes noces*.
'My mother with her pretty hair and youthful
shape . . . I watch her winding her bright curls round her
fingers, and straightening her waist.'—*David Copperfield*.

CORNEY, MRS. Matron of the workhouse where Oliver
Twist was born;
afterwards wife of
Mr. Bumble. 'It's no
part of my duty to
see all the old women
in the house die, and
I won't—that's more.
Mind that, you impu-
dent old harridans.'—
Oliver Twist.

Mrs. Corney and Mr. Bumble

CRACKIT, TOBY (FLASH TOBY). Housebreaker, partner
of Sikes. 'He had no very great quantity of hair . . . but
what he had was of a reddish dye and tortured into long
corkscrew curls, through which he occasionally thrust
some very dirty fingers.'—*Oliver Twist*.

CRAGGS. A lawyer. 'A cold, hard, dry man, dressed in
grey and white, like a flint, with small twinkles in his eyes,
as if something struck sparks out of them.'—*The Battle of
Life*.

CRATCHIT, BELINDA. One of Bob's daughters. 'Brave in ribbons.'—*A Christmas Carol*.

CRATCHIT, BOB. Scrooge's clerk. 'Bob had but fifteen "Bob" a week himself; he pocketed on Saturdays but fifteen copies of his Christian name, and yet the Ghost of Christmas Present blessed his four-roomed house.'—*A Christmas Carol*.

CRATCHIT, MRS. BOB. 'Dressed out but poorly in a twice turned gown, but brave in ribbons, which are cheap.' —*A Christmas Carol*.

CRATCHIT, MARTHA. Bob's elder daughter. 'Who was a poor apprentice at a milliner's.'—*A Christmas Carol*.

CRATCHIT, PETER. Their elder son. 'Looked thoughtfully at the fire, from between his collar, as if he were deliberating what particular investments he should favour . . .'—*A Christmas Carol*.

CRATCHIT, TIM. *See* TINY TIM—*A Christmas Carol*.

CREAKLE, MR. Head Master at Salem House. 'Mr. Creakle's face was fiery, and his eyes were small . . . he had a delight in cutting at the boys, which was like the satisfaction of a craving appetite.'—*David Copperfield*.

CREWLER, SOPHY. Daughter of the Rev. Horace Crewler, later the wife of Thomas Traddles. 'She has the most agreeable of faces—not absolutely beautiful—but extraordinarily pleasant—and is one of the most genial, unaffected, frank, engaging creatures I have ever seen.' —*David Copperfield*.

CRISPARKLE, MRS. Mother of the Rev. Septimus Crisparkle. 'What is prettier than an old lady . . . when her eyes are bright; when her figure is trim and compact . . . when her dress is the dress of a china shepherdess.' —*Edwin Drood.*

CRISPARKLE, REV. SEPTIMUS. Minor canon at Cloisterham Cathedral. 'Early riser; musical; classical; cheerful; kind; good-natured; social; contented; and boy-like.' —*Edwin Drood.*

CRUMMLES, MISS NINETTA. Ten-year-old daughter of Vincent Crummles. 'The infant phenomenon . . . the idol of every place we go into.'—*Nicholas Nickleby.*

CRUMMLES, VINCENT. Actor-manager of a company of strolling players. 'A hoarse voice, as though he were in the habit of shouting very much, and very short black hair, shaved off nearly to the crown of his head—to admit . . . of his more easily wearing character wigs of any shape or pattern.' —*Nicholas Nickleby.*

Vincent Crummles

CRUMMLES, MRS. VINCENT. 'A stout portly female . . . between forty and fifty, in a tarnished silk cloak.'—*Nicholas Nickleby.*

CRUNCHER, JERRY. Bank messenger and resurrectionist. 'He had eyes . . . that had a sinister expression, under an old cocked-hat like a three-cornered spittoon.'—*A Tale of Two Cities*.

CRUNCHER, JERRY, JUNIOR. 'A grisly urchin of twelve.' —*A Tale of Two Cities*.

CRUNCHER, MRS. JERRY. 'A woman of orderly and industrious appearance.'—*A Tale of Two Cities*.

CRUPP, MRS. David Copperfield's landlady at the Adelphi. 'A stout lady with a flounce of flannel petticoat below a nankeen gown.'—*David Copperfield*.

CUTE, ALDERMAN. Patron of Trotty Veck. 'A gentleman upon the smooth down-hill of life, wearing creaking boots, a watch-chain, and clean linen.'—*The Chimes*.

CUTTLE, CAPTAIN. Ex-naval man and friend of Solomon Gills. 'A gentleman in a wide suit of blue, with a hook instead of a hand attached to his right wrist . . . one of those timber-looking men, suits of oak as well as hearts.'—*Dombey and Son*.

Captain Cuttle

DAISY, SOLOMON. Parish clerk of Chigwell. ' . . . little queer buttons, like nothing except his eyes; but so like them, as they twinkled and glistened in the light of the fire . . . he seemed all eyes from head to foot.'—*Barnaby Rudge*.

DARNAY, CHARLES. English name of
Charles St. Evremonde, an exile from France,
later husband of Lucie Manette. 'Well-
grown and well-looking, with a sunburnt
cheek and a dark eye.'—*A Tale of Two Cities.*

*Charles
Darnay*

DARTLE, MISS ROSA. Companion to Mrs.
Steerforth. 'She had black hair and eager
eyes, and was thin . . . I concluded in my own mind
that she was about thirty years of age and that she wished
to be married.'—*David Copperfield.*

'DATCHERY, DICK'. Visitor to Cloisterham, disguised and
bent on detection; real identity unknown. 'A white-haired
personage with black eyebrows. He announced himself at
the Crozier . . . as an idle dog who lived upon his means.'
—*Edwin Drood.*

DAVID. Butler to the Brothers Cheeryble. 'Of apoplectic
appearance, and with very short legs.'—*Nicholas Nickleby.*

DAWKINS, JOHN ('THE ARTFUL DODGER'). One of
Fagin's gang of thieves. 'One of the queerest-looking boys
that Oliver had ever seen . . . he had about him all the airs
and manners of a man . . . altogether as roystering and
swaggering a young gentleman as ever stood four feet six,
or something less.'—*Oliver Twist.*

DEDLOCK, SIR LEICESTER, Baronet. 'Generally in a
complacent state, and rarely bored; when he has nothing
else to do, he can always contemplate his own greatness.'
—*Bleak House.*

DEDLOCK, LADY. Wife of Sir Leicester, and mother of
Esther Summerson. 'She had beauty, pride, ambition,

insolent resolve, and sense enough to
portion out a legion of fine ladies.'
—*Bleak House.*

DEDLOCK, MISS VOLUMNIA. Poor
relation of Sir Leicester. 'A young lady
(of sixty) who is doubly highly related.'
—*Bleak House.*

Lady Dedlock

DEFARGE, ERNEST. Wine-shop keeper of Paris, and
revolutionary. 'A bull-necked, martial-looking man of
thirty.'—*A Tale of Two Cities.*

DEFARGE, MADAME THERÈSE. His
wife. Leader of the women revolutionaries.
'A watchful eye that seldom seemed to look
at anything, a large hand heavily ringed, a
steady face . . . and great composure of
manner.'—*A Tale of Two Cities.*

*Madame
Therèse
Defarge*

DENHAM. Real name Edward Longford: a
poor student at the Institution where Redlaw
lectured. Nursed by Milly Swidger during
an illness. 'What change have you wrought in me? What
curse have you brought upon me? Give me back myself!'
—*The Haunted Man.*

DENNIS, NED. Hangman, and a leader in the Gordon
Riots. 'A squat, thick-set personage with a low retreating
forehead . . .'—*Barnaby Rudge.*

'DEPUTY.' Also known as 'Winks'. Boy employed at the
Travellers' lodging-house in Cloisterham. 'A hideous small
boy in rags, flinging stones . . .'—*Edwin Drood.*

DICK. A pauper child, friend of Oliver Twist. 'Pale and thin—his cheeks were sunken . . . his young limbs had wasted away like those of an old man.'—*Oliver Twist*.

'DICK, MR.' Mr. Richard Babley, who resided with Miss Betsey Trotwood. 'His head . . . curiously bowed—not by age . . . and his grey eyes prominent and large, with a strange kind of watery brightness in them, that made me . . . suspect him of being a little mad.'—*David Copperfield*.

DIOGENES. Dr. Blimber's dog, later the pet of Florence Dombey.'As ridiculous a dog as we could meet with on a summer's day; a blundering, ill-favoured, clumsy, bullet-headed dog . . . he was dearer to Florence . . . than the most valuable and beautiful of his kind.'—*Dombey and Son*.

'DISMAL JEMMY' (JEM HUTLEY). Brother of Job Trotter. Strolling player. 'A careworn-looking man.'—*The Pickwick Papers*.

DIVER, COLONEL. Editor of *The New York Rowdy Journal* encountered by Martin Chuzzlewit. 'A sallow gentleman, with sunken cheeks, black hair, small twinkling eyes, and a singular expression . . . which was not a frown, nor a leer, and yet might have been mistaken at the first glance for either.'—*Martin Chuzzlewit*.

DODSON, MR. Partner of the firm of Dodson and Fogg, Solicitors. 'A plump, portly, stern-looking man, with a loud voice.'—*The Pickwick Papers*.

DOLLOBY. Dealer in second-hand clothes. 'He looked like a man of revengeful disposition, who had hung all his enemies and was enjoying himself.'—*David Copperfield*.

DOMBEY, FLORENCE.
Daughter to Paul Dombey,
Senior. 'A dark-eyed little
girl.'—*Dombey and Son.*

DOMBEY, PAUL, JUNIOR.
(Portrait p. 136.) 'There
was something wan and
wistful in his small face,

Florence Dombey

that gave occasion to many significant shakes of
Mrs. Wickam's head.'—*Dombey and Son.*

DOMBEY, PAUL, SENIOR. 'About
eight-and-forty years of age . . .
rather bald, rather red, and though
a handsome, well-made man, too
stern and pompous in appearance
to be prepossessing.'—*Dombey and
Son.*

DOR, MADAME. Chaperone to
Marguerite Obenreizer. 'She was

Paul Dombey, Senior

a true Swiss impersonation . . . from the breadth of her
cushion-like back, and the ponderosity of her respectable
legs . . . to the black velvet band tied tightly round her
throat for the repression of a rising tendency to goitre.'—
No Thoroughfare.

DORRIT, AMY ('LITTLE DORRIT'). Sempstress, daughter of 'The Father of the Marshalsea'; later wife of
Arthur Clennam. 'A pale, transparent face, quick in
expression, though not beautiful in feature, its soft hazel
eyes excepted. A delicately bent head, a tiny form, a quick
little pair of busy hands, and a shabby dress . . . were Little
Dorrit as she sat at work.'—*Little Dorrit.*

DORRIT, EDWARD, JUNIOR ('TIP'). Brother of Little Dorrit. 'Tip tired of everything.'—*Little Dorrit*.

DORRIT, FANNY. Sister of Little Dorrit. 'A pretty girl, of a far better figure and much more developed than Little Dorrit.'—*Little Dorrit*.

DORRIT, WILLIAM. 'Father of the Marshalsea' and of Little Dorrit. 'A shy, retiring man; well-looking, though in an effeminate style . . . the shabby old debtor with the soft manner and the white hair.'—*Little Dorrit*.

DOWLER, MR. Traveller to Bath with the Pickwickians. 'A stern-eyed man of about five-and-forty, . . . with a good deal of black hair . . . and large black whiskers.' —*Pickwick Papers*.

DOWLER, MRS. Wife to Mr. Dowler. 'A rather pretty face in a bright blue bonnet.'—*The Pickwick Papers*.

DOYCE, DANIEL. An inventor. 'He . . . had the appearance of a sagacious master in some handicraft.'—*Little Dorrit*.

DROOD, EDWIN. An orphan, nephew to John Jasper, betrothed to Rosa Bud. His mysterious disappearance is unsolved when the unfinished book ends. 'I am afraid I am but a shallow surface kind of fellow Jack . . . but I needn't say I am young, and perhaps I shall not grow worse as I grow older.' —*The Mystery of Edwin Drood*.

Edwin Drood

DRUMMLE, BENTLEY. Fellow-pupil with Pip, at Matthew Pocket's, afterwards married to Estella. 'Heavy in figure, movement, and comprehension ... idle, proud, niggardly, reserved and suspicious.'—*Great Expectations*.

DURDLES. Stonemason at Cloisterham. 'Chiefly in the gravestone tomb and monument way, and wholly of their colour from head to foot.'—*Edwin Drood*.

Durdles

'EM'LY, LITTLE.' Niece of Daniel Peggotty, later mistress of Steerforth. 'She was a little creature still in stature, though she was grown. But when I ... saw her blue eyes looking bluer, and ... her whole self prettier and gayer, a curious feeling came over me that made me pretend not to know her.'—*David Copperfield*.

ENDELL, MARTHA. A prostitute, friend of Little Em'ly. 'It's a young woman, sir—that Em'ly knowed once, and doen't ought to know no more.'—*David Copperfield*.

ESTELLA. Adopted daughter of Miss Havisham, later wife of Bentley Drummle. 'The young lady, who was very pretty and seemed very proud.'—*Great Expectations*.

Fagin

FAGIN. Receiver of stolen property and head of the gang of thieves into which Oliver Twist was recruited. 'A very old shrivelled Jew, whose villainous-looking and repulsive face was obscured by a quantity, of matted red hair.'—*Oliver Twist.*

FAN. Scrooge's little sister. 'Always a delicate creature whom a breath might have withered, said the Ghost, but she had a large heart.'—*A Christmas Carol.*

FANG, MR. Magistrate. 'A lean, long-backed, stiff-necked, middle-sized man. If he were not in the habit of drinking rather more than was exactly good for him, he might have brought an action against his countenance for libel, and have recovered heavy damages.'—*Oliver Twist.*

FAT BOY THE, *See* 'JOE'—*The Pickwick Papers.*

FEEDER, MR. B.A. Dr. Blimber's assistant; later married Cornelia Blimber. 'A kind of human barrel-organ, with a little list of tunes, at which he was continually working over and over again.'—*Dombey and Son.*

FEENIX, LORD. Cousin of Edith Dombey. 'A man about town, forty years ago, but still so juvenile in figure . . . ' —*Dombey and Son.*

FERN, WILL. A poor countryman. 'Being found at night asleep in a shed was taken into custody and carried next morning before the Alderman.'—*The Chimes.*

FEZZIWIG, MR. Merchant with whom Scrooge served his apprenticeship. 'An old gentleman in a Welsh wig.'—*A Christmas Carol.*

FEZZIWIG, MRS. 'One vast substantial smile.'—*A Christmas Carol.*

FIELDING, MAY. Friend of Dot Peerybingle .'May was very pretty.'—*The Cricket on the Hearth.*

FIELDING, MRS. Mother of May. 'A little querulous chip of an old lady with a peevish face.'—*The Cricket on the Hearth.*

FILER, MR. Friend of Alderman Cute. 'A low-spirited gentleman of middle-age, of a meagre habit.'—*The Chimes.*

FINCHING, FLORA. Sweetheart of Arthur Clennam in boyhood. 'Flora, always tall, had grown to be very broad too, and short of breath . . . Flora, who had been spoiled and artless long ago, was determined to be spoiled and artless now.'—*Little Dorrit.*

Flora Finching

FIPS. MR. Solicitor of Austin Friars, employed by old Martin Chuzzlewit. 'Small and spare, and looked peaceable, and wore black shorts and powder.'—*Martin Chuzzlewit.*

FISH, MR. Secretary to Sir Joseph Bowley. 'A not very stately gentleman in black.'—*The Chimes.*

FIZKIN, HORATIO. Buff candidate for Eatanswill, defeated by Slumkey. 'A tall thin gentleman, in a stiff white neckerchief.'—*The Pickwick Papers.*

FLEDGEBY. Moneylender. 'He was the meanest cur existing with a single pair of legs. Fascination Fledgeby feigned to be a young gentleman living on his means; but was known secretly to be a kind of outlaw in the bill-broking line.'—*Our Mutual Friend.*

FLEMING, AGNES. Mother of Oliver Twist and sister of Rose Maylie. 'The old story . . . no wedding-ring, I see.' —*Oliver Twist*.

FLINTWINCH, JEREMIAH. Confidential clerk, afterwards partner, of Clennam and Co. Husband of Mrs. Clennam's maid Affery. 'A short, bald old man . . . he had a one-sided crab-like way with him.'—*Little Dorrit*.

Mr. and Mrs. Flintwinch

FLINTWINCH, MRS. *See* AFFERY—*Little Dorrit*.

FLITE, MISS. Eccentric character haunting the Law Courts. 'A curious little old woman, in a squeezed bonnet.' —*Bleak House*.

FLOWERS. Maid to Mrs. Skewton. 'At night, she should have been a skeleton, with dart and hour-glass, rather than a woman, this attendant; for her touch was as the touch of Death.' —*Dombey and Son*.

FOGG. MR. Partner in the firm of Dodson and Fogg, Solicitors. 'An elderly, pimply-faced, vegetable-diet sort of man . . . a kind of being who seemed to be an essential part of the desk at which he was writing.'—*The Pickwick Papers*.

Miss Flite

FOLAIR, MR. Comedian in Mr. Crummles' company. 'Mr. Folair made a funny face from his pantomime collection.'—*Nicholas Nickleby*.

FRED. Nephew of Scrooge. 'If you should happen by any unlikely chance to know a man more blest in a laugh . . . all I can say is I should like to know him too.'—*A Christmas Carol.*

FRED. MRS. Scrooge's niece by marriage. 'A ripe little mouth that seemed made to be kissed, as no doubt it was; all kinds of good little dots about her chin.'—*A Christmas Carol.*

'GAME CHICKEN, THE.' Pugilist friend of Mr. Toots. 'A stoical gentleman, in a shaggy white great coat, . . . and a considerable tract of bare and sterile country behind each ear.'—*Dombey and Son.*

GAMFIELD. A chimney-sweep. 'His villainous countenance was a stamped receipt for cruelty.'—*Oliver Twist.*

GAMP, MRS. SARAH. Nurse and midwife. 'She was a fat old woman . . . with a husky voice and a moist eye . . . The

Betsey Prig and Sarah Gamp

face of Mrs. Gamp—the nose in particular—was somewhat red and swollen, and it was difficult to enjoy her society without becoming conscious of a smell of spirits.'—*Martin Chuzzlewit.*

GARGERY, JOE. Blacksmith; brother-in-law to Pip (Philip Pirrip). 'He was a mild, good-natured, easy-going, sweet-tempered, foolish, dear fellow—a sort of Hercules in strength and also in weakness.'—*Great Expectations.*

GARGERY, MRS. JOE. Pip's sister. 'She . . . had such a prevailing redness of skin that I sometimes used to wonder whether it was possible she washed herself with a nutmeg-grater instead of soap.'—*Great Expectations.*

GARLAND, ABEL. Articled clerk to Mr. Witherden, son of Mr. and Mrs. Garland. ' . . . had a quaint old-fashioned air about him, looked nearly of the same age as his father . . . '—*The Old Curiosity Shop.*

GARLAND, MR. Kit Nubbles' benefactor. 'A little, fat, placid old gentleman.'—*The Old Curiosity Shop.*

GARLAND, MRS. 'A little old lady, plump and placid like himself.'—*The Old Curiosity Shop.*

GASHFORD. Secretary to Lord George Gordon. 'He wore the aspect of a man who was always lying in wait for something that *wouldn't* come to pass.'—*Barnaby Rudge.*

GAY, WALTER. Nephew of Solomon Gills, clerk in Dombey and Son's counting house; later married to Florence Dombey. 'A cheerful-looking merry boy . . . fair faced, bright eyed, and curly haired.'—*Dombey and Son.*

GENERAL, MRS. Companion of the Misses Dorrit. 'If she had few wrinkles it was because her mind had never traced its name, or any other inscription, on her face.'—*Little Dorrit*.

GENTLEMAN IN SMALL-CLOTHES, THE. The Nickle-bys' mad neighbour at Bow, would-be suitor of Mrs. Nickleby. (Portrait p. 123.) 'I have estates, ma'am, . . . jewels, lighthouses, fish-ponds, a whalery of my own in the North Sea, and several oyster-beds of great profit in the Pacific Ocean. If you will have the kindness to step down to the Royal Exchange and to take the cocked hat off the stoutest beadle's head, you will find my card in the lining of the crown.'—*Nicholas Nickleby*.

GEORGE. Driver of Mrs. Jarley's touring-van, later her husband. 'A man in a carter's frock.'—*The Old Curiosity Shop*.

GILES, MR. Butler and steward to Mrs. Maylie at Chertsey. 'Towards the humbler servants it was rather his wont to deport himself with a lofty affability, which, while it gratified, could not fail to remind them of his superior position in society.'—*Oliver Twist*.

GILLS, SOLOMON. Nautical instrument seller, uncle of Walter Gay. 'He was a slow, quiet spoken, thoughtful old fellow, with eyes as red as if they had been small suns looking at you through a fog, and a newly awakened manner.'—*Dombey and Son*.

GLUBB, OLD. Chair-wheeler at Brighton. 'He knows all about the deep sea, and the fish that are in it, and the great monsters that come and lie on the rocks in the sun.' —*Dombey and Son*.

GOLDSTRAW, MRS. SARAH. Nurse at the Foundlings' Hospital, later housekeeper at Cripple Corner. 'A woman perhaps fifty, but looking younger . . . with a face remarkable for its quiet expression of equability of temper.'—*No Thoroughfare*.

GORDON, LORD GEORGE. President of the Protestant Association. 'His very large bright eye . . . betrayed a restlessness of thought and purpose singularly at variance with the studied composure and sobriety of his mien.'—*Barnaby Rudge*.

Lord George Gordon

GOWAN, HENRY. Artist, later husband of Minnie Meagles. 'He was well dressed, of a sprightly and gay appearance.'—*Little Dorrit*.

GRADGRIND, LOUISA. Thomas Gradgrind's daughter, later wife of Bounderby. 'She was pretty; would have been self-willed . . . but for her bringing up.'—*Hard Times*.

GRADGRIND, THOMAS. Retired merchant. 'A kind of cannon loaded to the muzzle with facts.'—*Hard Times*.

GRADGRIND, MRS. THOMAS. 'A little, thin, white, pink-eyed bundle of shawls.'—*Hard Times*.

GRADGRIND, TOM ('THE WHELP'). Their son. 'I am a donkey—that's what I am.'—*Hard Times*.

GRAHAM, MARY. Companion of old Martin Chuzzlewit, later wife of Martin the younger. 'With a greater share of self-possession and control over her emotions than usually belongs to a far more advanced period of female life.' —*Martin Chuzzlewit*.

GRANGER, MRS. EDITH. Daughter of Mrs. Skewton, later the second Mrs. Dombey. 'Very handsome, very haughty, very wilful.'—*Dombey and Son.*

GREGSBURY, MR. Member of Parliament to whom Nicholas applied for the post of private secretary. 'A tough, burly, thick-headed gentleman, with a loud voice, a pompous manner, a tolerable command of sentences with no meaning in them.'—*Nicholas Nickleby.*

GREWGIOUS, HIRAM. Lawyer, of Staple Inn, and guardian of Rosa Bud. 'He was an arid sandy man; who, if he had been put into a grinding mill, looked as if he would have ground immediately into high-dried snuff.' —*Edwin Drood.*

Hiram Grewgious

GRIDE, ARTHUR. Moneylender. 'The whole expression of the face was concentrated in a wrinkled leer, compounded of cunning, lecherousness, slyness, and avarice.' —*Nicholas Nickleby.*

GRIMWIG, MR. Friend of Mr. Brownlow. 'A stout old gentleman, rather lame in one leg.'—*Oliver Twist.*

GRIP. A talking raven, companion of Barnaby Rudge. ' . . . listened with polite attention, and a most extraordinary appearance of comprehending every word.' —*Barnaby Rudge.*

GROVES, JEM. Landlord of 'The Valiant Soldier.' 'Honest Jem Groves—as is a man of unblemished moral character, and has a good dry skittle ground.'—*The Old Curiosity Shop.*

GRUB, GABRIEL. Central figure in Mr. Wardle's story. 'An ill-conditioned cross-grained surly fellow . . . who consorted with nobody but himself and an old wicker bottle.'—*The Pickwick Papers*.

GRUDDEN, MRS. Member of Mr. Crummles' company. 'Who . . . was put down in the bills under any name or names whatever that occurred to Mr. Crummles as looking well in print.'—*Nicholas Nickleby*.

GRUEBY, JOHN. Servant to Lord George Gordon. 'A square-built strong-made, bull-necked fellow of the true English breed.'—*Barnaby Rudge*.

GRUMMER. Officer to the Ipswich magistrate. 'Chiefly remarkable for a bottle nose; a hoarse voice; a snuff-coloured surtout; and a wandering eye.'—*The Pickwick Papers*.

GUMMIDGE, MRS. Housekeeper to Daniel Peggotty; a widow. 'A lone lorn creetur.'—*David Copperfield*.

GUPPY, MR. Clerk to Kenge and Carboy. 'A young gentleman, who had inked himself by accident.' —*Bleak House*.

GUPPY, MRS. Mother of Mr. Guppy. 'She has her failings—as who has not—but I never knew her do it when

Mr. Guppy

company was present, at which time you may freely trust her with wines, spirits, or malt liquors.'—*Bleak House*.

GUSTER. Mrs. Snagsby's maid. 'Aged three or four-and twenty, but looking a round ten years older, goes cheap with this unaccountable drawback of fits.'—*Bleak House*.

HANDFORD, JULIUS. *See* HARMON, JOHN—*Our Mutual Friend*.

HAREDALE, EMMA. Niece of Geoffrey Haredale, later married to Edward Chester. 'A lovely girl.'—*Barnaby Rudge*.

HAREDALE, GEOFFREY. A Roman Catholic gentleman. 'A burly, square-built man, negligently dressed, rough and abrupt in manner.' —*Barnaby Rudge*.

Emma Haredale

HARMON, JOHN. Alias Julius Handford and John Rokesmith. Son and heir of a dust contractor, later husband of Bella Wilfer. 'A boy of spirit and resource.'— *Our Mutual Friend*.

HARRIS, *See* SHORT.—*The Old Curiosity Shop*.

HARRIS, MRS. Imaginary friend of Mrs. Gamp. 'A fearful mystery surrounded this lady of the name of Harris.' —*Martin Chuzzlewit*.

HARRY. Favourite pupil of Mr. Marton. 'His eyes were very bright; but their light was of heaven, not of earth.' —*The Old Curiosity Shop*.

HARTHOUSE, JAMES. Man of the world; friend of Mr. Gradgrind. Attempted to seduce Louisa Bounderby. 'Five-and-thirty, good-looking, good figure, good teeth, good voice, good breeding.'—*Hard Times*.

HAVISHAM, MISS. Once engaged to Compeyson; later guardian of Estella. 'The bride within the bridal dress had withered like the dress, and like the flowers.'—*Great Expectations*.

HAWDON, CAPTAIN (alias Nemo). Lover of Lady Dedlock and father of Esther Summerson; a law-writer lodging at Mr. Krook's. 'His hair is ragged, mingling with his whiskers and his beard . . . dressed in shirt and trousers with bare feet.'—*Bleak House*.

HAWK, SIR MULBERRY. Man of the world and tool of Ralph Nickleby. 'Another superlative gentleman, something older, something stouter, and something redder in the face . . .'—*Nicholas Nickleby*.

HEADSTONE, BRADLEY. School-teacher, unsuccessful suitor of Lizzie Hexham. 'It was a face belonging to a naturally slow or inattentive intellect.'—*Our Mutual Friend*.

HEATHFIELD, ALFRED. Betrothed of Marion Jeddler, but later husband of her sister Grace. 'A handsome young man . . . with an air of gaiety and hope that accorded well with the morning.'—*The Battle of Life*.

HEEP, URIAH. Mr. Wickfield's clerk, later his partner. ' . . . whose hair was cropped as close as the closest stubble, who had hardly any eyebrows, and no eyelashes, and eyes of a red brown, so unsheltered and unshaded that I remember wondering how he went to sleep.'—*David Copperfield*.

Uriah Heep

HEEP, MRS. Mother of Uriah. 'Who was the dead image of Uriah, only short.'—*David Copperfield*.

HEXAM, CHARLEY. Son of Gaffer Hexam. 'There was a curious mixture in the boy, of uncompleted savagery, and uncompleted civilization.'—*Our Mutual Friend*.

HEXAM, JESSE ('GAFFER'). Riverside body searcher. 'A strong man with ragged, grizzled hair, and a sunbrowned face.'—*Our Mutual Friend*.

HEXAM, LIZZIE. Daughter of Gaffer Hexam, later wife of Eugene Wrayburn. 'A dark girl of nineteen or twenty.' —*Our Mutual Friend*.

HIGDEN, MRS. BETTY. Great-grandmother of Johnny, the orphan adopted by the Boffins. 'An active old woman, with a bright dark eye, and a resolute face, yet quite a tender creature too.'—*Our Mutual Friend*.

HOMINY, MRS. American authoress. 'She certainly could not be considered young—that was matter of fact; and probably could not be considered handsome—but that was matter of opinion.'—*Martin Chuzzlewit*.

HONEYTHUNDER, LUKE. Chairman of the Haven of Philanthropy. 'His philanthropy was of that gunpowderous sort that the difference between it and animosity was hard to determine.'—*Edwin Drood*.

HOPKINS, CAPTAIN. Debtor in the King's Bench Prison at the same time as the Micawbers. 'In the last extremity of shabbiness, with large whiskers, and an old, old brown greatcoat with no other coat below it.'—*David Copperfield*.

HOPKINS, JACK. Medical student from St. Bartholomew's Hospital. Friend of Bob Sawyer and Ben Allen. 'He wore a black velvet waistcoat, with thunder-and-lightning buttons.'—*The Pickwick Papers*.

HORTENSE. Lady Dedlock's French maid. 'She seems to go about like a very neat She-Wolf, imperfectly tamed.' —*Bleak House.*

HOWLER, REV. MELCHISEDECH. Minister of the Ranting persuasion, and Mrs. MacStinger's spiritual adviser. He married her to Captain Bunsby. 'Having been one day discharged from the West India Docks on a false suspicion . . . of screwing gimlets into puncheons and applying his lips to the orifice.'—*Dombey and Son.*

HUBBLE. A wheelwright. 'A tough high-shouldered stooping old man, of a sawdusty fragrance, with his legs extraordinarily wide apart.'—*Great Expectations.*

HUGH. Ostler at the Maypole Inn; natural son of Sir John Chester. 'A young man of a hale athletic figure, and a giant's strength, whose sunburnt face and swarthy throat, overgrown with jet black hair, might have served a painter for a model.'—*Barnaby Rudge.*

HUMM, ANTHONY. President of the Brick Lane Branch of the United Grand Junction Ebenezer Temperance Association. 'A sleek, white-faced man in a perpetual perspiration.'—*The Pickwick Papers.*

HUNTER, MRS. LEO. Literary lady and hostess. 'She dotes on poetry, sir. She adores it.'—*The Pickwick Papers.*

HUTLEY, JEM. *See* 'DISMAL JEMMY'—*The Pickwick Papers.*

JAGGERS, MR. A criminal lawyer. 'With an exceedingly large head and a correspondingly large hand.'—*Great Expectations.*

JANET. Miss Betsey Trotwood's servant. 'A pretty blooming girl . . . and a perfect picture of neatness.'—*David Copperfield*.

JARLEY, MRS. Proprietor of a travelling waxwork show. 'A Christian lady, stout and comfortable to look upon.'—*The Old Curiosity Shop*.

JARNDYCE, JOHN. Owner of Bleak House. 'It was a handsome, lively, quick face, full of change and motion.'—*Bleak House*.

Mrs. Jarley

JASPER, JOHN. Lay Precentor at Cloisterham Cathedral. Uncle of Edwin Drood. 'His voice is deep and good, his face and figure are good, his manner is a little sombre.'—*Edwin Drood*.

John Jasper

JEDDLER, DOCTOR. Father of Grace and Marion. 'The heart and mystery of his philosophy was to look upon the world as a gigantic practical joke.'—*The Battle of Life*.

JEDDLER, GRACE. Doctor Jeddler's elder daughter. 'The home-adorning, self-denying qualities of Grace, and her sweet temper, so gentle and retiring . . . '—*The Battle of Life*.

JEDDLER, MARION. Grace's younger sister. 'So beautiful, so happy . . . so elevated and exalted in her loveliness.' —*The Battle of Life.*

JELLYBY, MRS. Devotee of African mission work, and especially of the natives of Borrioboola Gha. 'Had very good hair, but was too much occupied with her African duties to brush it.'—*Bleak House.*

JELLYBY, CAROLINE ('CADDY'). Daughter and secretary of Mrs. Jellyby. 'I suppose nobody ever was in such a state of ink.'—*Bleak House.*

JENNY. Wife of a drunken brickmaker. Lady Dedlock changed clothes with her during her flight to London. 'A woman with a black eye, nursing a poor little gasping baby by the fire.'—*Bleak House.*

Caroline Jellyby

JINGLE, ALFRED. Strolling player and gentleman of

Alfred Jingle and Dr. Slammer

fortune. 'His face was thin and haggard, but an indescribable air of jaunty impudence and perfect self-possession pervaded the whole man.'—*The Pickwick Papers.*

JINIWIN, MRS. Mother of Mrs. Quilp. 'Known to be laudably shrewdish in her disposition, and inclined to resist male authority.'—*The Old Curiosity Shop.*

JINKINS, MR. Senior boarder at Mrs. Todgers'. 'Of a fashionable turn, being a regular frequenter of the Park on Sundays.'—*Martin Chuzzlewit.*

JINKINS, MR. Admirer of the landlady at an inn at Marlborough Downs, rival of Tom Smart. 'A tall man—a very tall man—in a brown coat and bright basket buttons.' —The Bagman's Story, *The Pickwick Papers.*

JIP. Dora Spenlow's dog. 'Got under a chair expressly to snarl, and wouldn't hear of the least familiarity.'—*David Copperfield.*

JO. A boy crossing-sweeper. 'He knows that it is hard to keep the mud off the crossing in dirty weather, and harder still to live by doing it.'—*Bleak House.*

JOBLING, TONY. Friend of Mr. Guppy. 'He has the faded appearance of a gentleman in embarrassed circumstances.' —*Bleak House.*

JOBLING, DOCTOR. Medical Officer of the Anglo-Bengalee Insurance Company. 'He had a portentously sagacious chin.'—*Martin Chuzzlewit.*

JOE ('THE FAT BOY'). Page to Mr. Wardle. 'The leaden eyes, which twinkled behind his mountainous cheeks, leered horribly upon the food.'—*The Pickwick Papers*.

JOHNNY. Great-grandchild of Betty Higden. 'He's a pretty boy; he's a dear darling boy.'—*Our Mutual Friend*.

Joe 'The Fat Boy'

JORAM. Assistant to Mr. Omer, the undertaker. 'A good-looking young fellow.'—*David Copperfield*.

JORKINS, MR. Partner of Spenlow and Jorkins. 'A mild man of a heavy temperament, whose place in the business was to keep himself in the background.'—*David Copperfield*.

JUPE, 'SIGNOR'. Clown in Sleary's Circus. ' . . . was to enliven the varied performances . . . with his chaste Shakespearean quips and retorts.'—*Hard Times*.

JUPE, CISSY. His daughter, became servant to Gradgrind. 'So dark-eyed, and dark-haired, that she seemed to receive a deeper and more lustrous colour from the sun.'—*Hard Times*.

KAGS. A convict. 'Whose nose had almost been beaten in some old scuffle.'—*Oliver Twist*.

KENGE, MR. ('CONVERSATION'). Of the firm of Kenge and Carboy, solicitors. 'A portly, important-looking gentleman dressed all in black . . . he appeared to enjoy beyond everything the sound of his own voice.'—*Bleak House*.

KENWIGS, MR. A turner in ivory. First-
floor tenant at Newman Noggs' lodgings.
'Looked upon as a person of some con-
sideration on the premises.'—*Nicholas
Nickleby*.

KENWIGS, MISS MORLEENA. His
eldest daughter. 'Had flaxen hair tied
with blue ribands hanging in luxuriant pig-
tails . . . and wore little white trousers with
frills round the ankles.'—*Nicholas Nickleby*.

*Morleena
Kenwigs*

KENWIGS, MRS. SUSAN. Wife of Mr. Kenwigs. 'Quite a
lady in her manners.'—*Nicholas Nickleby*.

KIBBLE, JACOB. Witness at the inquest on Harmon's
body. 'There's the mercantile cut upon him which would
make you happy to give him credit for five hundred
pounds.'—*Our Mutual Friend*.

KIDGERBURY, MRS. Temporary servant of the young
Copperfields. 'The oldest inhabitant of Kentish Town.'
—*David Copperfield*.

KNAG, MISS. Forewoman at Madame Mantalini's. 'Still
aimed at youth although she had shot beyond it years ago.'
—*Nicholas Nickleby*.

KNAG, MORTIMER. Brother of Miss Knag. 'Garnished
with much less hair than a gentleman bordering on forty
. . . usually boasts.'—*Nicholas Nickleby*.

KROOK. Rag and bone dealer. 'Short, cadaverous and
withered . . . like some old root in a fall of snow.'—*Bleak
House*.

LA CREEVY, MISS. Miniature-portrait painter. 'A mincing young lady of fifty.'—*Nicholas Nickleby*.

LADLE, JOEY. Head cellarman of Wilding and Co. 'A slow and ponderous man, of the drayman order of human architecture.'— *No Thoroughfare*.

LADY JANE. Mr. Krook's cat. 'I deal in cat-skins among other general matters and hers was offered

Miss La Creevy

to me. It's a very fine skin, as you may see, but I didn't have it stripped off !'—*Bleak House*.

LAMMLE, ALFRED. A professional adventurer. 'A mature young gentleman with too much nose on his face . . . too much sparkle in his studs, his eyes, his buttons, his talk and his teeth.'—*Our Mutual Friend*.

LANDLESS, NEVILLE AND HELENA. Twins, wards of Mr. Honeythunder. 'A certain air upon them of hunter and huntress; yet, withal, a certain air of being the objects of the chase, rather than the followers.'—*Edwin Drood*.

Helena Landless

LARKINS, THE ELDEST MISS. Early inamorata of David Copperfield. 'Not a little girl. She is a tall, dark, black-eyed fine figure of a woman.'—*David Copperfield*.

LEEFORD, EDWARD. Alias Monks. Half-brother of Oliver Twist. 'A dark figure . . . '—*Oliver Twist*.

LENVILLE, MR. Tragedian in Mr. Crummles' company. 'His face was long, and very pale, from the constant application of stage paint.'—*Nicholas Nickleby*.

LEWSOME, MR. Doctor's assistant. 'A young man—dark and not ill-looking.'—*Martin Chuzzlewit*.

LIGHTWOOD, MORTIMER. Solicitor, friend of Eugene Wrayburn. 'Who sits disconsolate on Mrs. Veneering's left, and who was inveigled . . . to come to these people's and talk, and won't talk.'—*Our Mutual Friend*.

LILLYVICK, MR. Uncle of Mrs. Kenwigs, later married to Miss Petowker. 'With a face that might have been carved out of lignum vitae, for anything that appeared to the contrary.'—*Nicholas Nickleby*.

Mr. Lillyvick

LILIAN. Niece of Will Fern, later a prostitute in Trotty's dream. 'In the long silken hair he saw the self-same curls; around the lips the child's expression lingering still.' —*The Chimes*.

LIMBKINS, MR. Chairman of the parochial board. 'A particularly fat gentleman with a very round red face.' —*Oliver Twist*.

LINKINWATER, TIM. Book-keeper and confidential clerk to the Cheeryble Brothers; later married Miss La Creevy. 'Punctual as the Counting House Dial.'—*Nicholas Nickleby*.

LINKINWATER, MISS. Sister of Tim. 'The chubby old lady.'—*Nicholas Nickleby*.

LION. Henry Gowan's dog—'A fine Newfoundland.' —*Little Dorrit*.

'LION, THE BLACK.' Landlord of the Black Lion Tavern. 'Stood indebted in no small amount to beer.'—*Barnaby Rudge*.

LITTIMER. Steerforth's valet. 'Such a self-contained man I never saw.'—*David Copperfield*.

LOBBS, OLD. A saddler in the tale of 'The Parish Clerk' told to Mr. Pickwick. 'Who could have bought up the whole village at one stroke of his pen.'—*The Pickwick Papers*.

LOBBS, MARIA. His daughter. 'A prettier foot, a gayer heart, a more dimpled face, or a smarter form, never bounded so lightly over the earth they graced.'—*The Pickwick Papers*.

LOBLEY. Boatman to Lieutenant Tartar. 'He was the dead image of the sun in old woodcuts; his hair and whiskers answering for rays all round him.'—*Edwin Drood*.

LORRY, MR. JARVIS. Confidential representative of Tellson's Bank. 'A face, habitually suppressed and quieted, was still lighted up under the quaint wig by a pair of moist bright eyes.'—*A Tale of Two Cities*.

LOSBERNE, DOCTOR. A doctor attending at Mrs. Maylie's. 'As kind and hearty, and withal as eccentric an old bachelor, as will be found . . .'—*Oliver Twist*.

LOWTEN, MR. Clerk to Mr. Perker. 'A puffy-faced young man.'—*The Pickwick Papers*.

LUMBEY, DOCTOR. Doctor to Mrs. Kenwigs. 'With no shirt collar to speak of, and a beard that had been growing since yesterday morning.'—*Nicholas Nickleby*.

LUPIN, MRS. Landlady of the Blue Dragon. 'In full bloom she was now, with roses on her ample skirts . . . and roses worth the gathering, too, on her lips for that matter.' —*Martin Chuzzlewit*.

M'CHOAKUMCHILD, MR. Teacher in Gradgrind's Model School. 'If only he had learnt a little less, how infinitely better he might have taught much more!' —*Hard Times*.

MACSTINGER, MRS. Captain Cuttle's landlady. 'With her sleeves rolled up to her shoulders, and her arms frothy with soap suds.'—*Dombey and Son*.

MAGGY. Grand-daughter of Mrs. Bangham, a girl of retarded development. 'With large bones, large features, large feet and hands, large eyes, and no hair.' —*Little Dorrit*.

Maggy

MAGNUS, PETER. Traveller to Ipswich with Mr. Pickwick. 'With a bird-like habit of giving his head a jerk every time he said anything.'—*The Pickwick Papers*.

MAGWITCH, ABEL. Escaped convict, later benefactor of Pip. 'A fearful man, all in coarse grey, with a great iron on his leg.'—*Great Expectations*.

MALDON, JACK. Cousin of Mrs. Strong. 'Sneering at the hand that gave it him, and speaking to me of the Doctor as so charmingly antique.'—*David Copperfield.*

MANETTE, DOCTOR. Father of Lucie; a Paris doctor long imprisoned in the Bastille. 'A white head bent low over the shoemaking . . .'—*A Tale of Two Cities.*

MANETTE, LUCIE. Daughter of Doctor Manette, later wife of Charles Darnay. 'A short, slight, pretty figure, a quantity of golden hair, a pair of blue eyes that met his own with an enquiring look . . .'—*A Tale of Two Cities.*

Dr. Manette

MANN, MRS. Matron of a parish branch workhouse. 'She knew what was good for children; and she had a very accurate perception of what was good for herself.'—*Oliver Twist.*

MANTALINI, MADAME. Head of a dressmaking establishment. 'A buxom person, handsomely dressed, and rather good-looking, but much older than the gentleman whom she had wedded.' —*Nicholas Nickleby.*

MANTALINI, ALFRED. Husband of Madame Mantalini. Originally Muntle. 'He had married on his whiskers.' —*Nicholas Nickleby.*

Alfred Mantalini

MARCHIONESS, THE. Servant at Sampson Brass's, later the wife of Dick Swiveller, christened by him 'Sophronia Sphinx'. 'A small, slipshod girl, in a dirty coarse apron and bib.'—*The Old Curiosity Shop.*

MARKHAM. Friend of Steerforth. 'He always spoke of himself indefinitely as—a man—and seldom or never in the first person singular.'—*David Copperfield.*

The Marchioness

MARKLEHAM, MRS. Mother of Mrs. Strong. 'Our boys used to call her The Old Soldier, on account of her generalship. She . . . used to wear when she was dressed one unchangeable cap.'—*David Copperfield.*

MARLEY, JACOB. Scrooge's deceased partner, returned as a ghost. (Portrait, p. 157.) 'Scrooge had often heard it said that Marley had no bowels, but he had never believed it until now.'—*A Christmas Carol.*

MARTHA. Daughter of a riverside labourer. 'Ugly, misshapen, peevish, ill-conditioned, fagged, dirty—but beloved!'—*Dombey and Son.*

MARTIN, JACK. The Bagman's uncle, in his story told to Mr. Pickwick. 'One of the merriest, pleasantest, cleverest fellows that ever lived.'—*The Pickwick Papers.*

MARTON, MR. A village school-master. 'A pale, simple-looking man, of a spare and meagre habit.'—*The Old Curiosity Shop.*

MARWOOD, ALICE. Daughter of 'Good Mrs. Brown', and James Carker's cast-off mistress. 'Tall; well-formed; handsome; miserably dressed . . . nothing to defend her rich black hair from the rain, but a torn handkerchief.' —*Dombey and Son*.

MARY. Housemaid at Mr. Nupkins', Ipswich, afterwards wife of Sam Weller. (Portrait, p. 102.) 'If I wos master o' this here house, I should alvays find the materials for comfort vere Mary wos.'—*The Pickwick Papers*.

MARY ANNE. Assistant and favourite pupil of Miss Peecher. 'Sufficiently divined the state of Miss Peecher's affections to feel it necessary that she herself should love young Charley Hexam.'—*Our Mutual Friend*.

MAYLIE, MRS. Resident of Chertsey, adopted aunt of Rose. 'The high-backed oaken chair in which she sat was not more upright than she.'—*Oliver Twist*.

MAYLIE, HARRY. Son of Mrs. Maylie, later married to Rose. 'His countenance was frank and handsome; and his demeanour easy and prepossessing.'—*Oliver Twist*.

MAYLIE, ROSE. Adopted niece of Mrs. Maylie, in reality Oliver's aunt. (Portrait, p. 67.) 'The changing expression of sweetness and good humour; the thousand lights that played about the face, and left no shadow there.'—*Oliver Twist*.

MEAGLES, MR. A retired banker. 'With a whimsical good humour on him all the time.'—*Little Dorrit*.

MEAGLES, MRS. 'Like Mr. Meagles, comely and healthy, with a pleasant English face . . . '—*Little Dorrit*.

MEAGLES, MINNIE ('PET'). Married Henry Gowan. 'She was round, and fresh, and dimpled, and spoilt.' —*Little Dorrit*.

MELL, MR. CHARLES. Second assistant at Salem House, later master of a school in Australia. 'A gaunt, sallow young man, with hollow cheeks.'—*David Copperfield*.

MERDLE, MR., M.P. A rich man. 'A somewhat uneasy expression about his coat cuffs, as if they were in his confidence, and had reasons for being anxious to hide his hands.'—*Little Dorrit*.

MERDLE, MRS. 'The lady was not young and fresh from the hand of Nature; but was young and fresh from the hand of her maid.'—*Little Dorrit*.

MICAWBER, MRS. EMMA. 'A thin and faded lady not at all young.'—*David Copperfield*.

MICAWBER, WILKINS. Friend of David Copperfield, chronically impecunious. 'His clothes were shabby, but he had an imposing shirt collar on . . . with no more hair upon his head (which was a large one and very shining) than there is upon an egg . . . '—*David Copperfield*.

Wilkins Micawber

MIFF, MRS. Pew-opener at a Marylebone Church. 'A mighty dry old lady . . . a vinegary face . . . and a mortified bonnet, and eke a thirsty soul for sixpences and shillings.' —*Dombey and Son*.

MIGGS, MISS. Servant of Mrs. Varden; later a turnkey at Bridewell. 'A tall young lady, very much addicted to pattens in private life, slender and shrewish, of a rather uncomfortable figure.'—*Barnaby Rudge*.

Miss Miggs

MILLS, JULIA. Friend of Dora Spenlow. 'Comparatively stricken in years— almost twenty I should say.'—*David Copperfield*.

MILVEY, REV. FRANK. A curate. 'Expensively educated and wretchedly paid.'—*Our Mutual Friend*.

MILVEY, MRS. ' . . . had repressed many pretty tastes and bright fancies, and substituted in their stead schools, soup, flannel, coals . . . '—*Our Mutual Friend*.

MODDLE, AUGUSTUS. Boarder at Mrs. Todgers', later narrowly escaped marriage with Charity Pecksniff. 'His spirit loves to hold communion with itself, and his soul recoils from noisy revellers.'—*Martin Chuzzlewit*.

MOLLY. Housekeeper to Mr. Jaggers, and mother of Estella. 'Extremely pale, with large faded eyes and a quantity of streaming hair.'—*Great Expectations*.

MONFLATHERS, MISS. Principal of a boarding-school for young ladies, solicited by little Nell to attend Jarley's Waxworks. 'Of a rather uncertain temper, and lost no opportunity of impressing moral truths upon the tender minds of the young ladies.'—*The Old Curiosity Shop*.

MORFIN, MR. Assistant-manager in Dombey and Son's counting house. 'A cheerful-looking, hazel-eyed, elderly bachelor . . . a great musical amateur in his way.'—*Dombey and Son*.

MOULD, MR. An undertaker. 'He looked as a man might, who in the very act of smacking his lips over choice old wine, tried to make believe it was physic.'—*Martin Chuzzlewit.*

MOULD, THE MISSES. His daughters. 'They might have been the bodies once belonging to the angels' faces in the shop below, grown up, with other heads attached.'—*Martin Chuzzlewit.*

MOWCHER, MISS. A dwarf beauty-specialist. (Portrait, p. 90.) 'A very large head and face, a pair of roguish grey eyes, and such extremely little arms . . .'—*David Copperfield.*

MURDSTONE, EDWARD. Second husband of Mrs. Copperfield, David's mother. (Portrait, p. 141.) 'He had that kind of shallow black eye . . . which, when it is abstracted, seems, from some peculiarity of light, to be disfigured for a moment at a time by a cast . . .'—*David Copperfield.*

MURDSTONE, MISS JANE. Mr. Murdstone's sister. (Portrait, p. 141.) 'Very heavy eyebrows nearly meeting over her large nose, as if, being disabled by the wrongs of her sex from wearing whiskers, she had carried them to that account.'—*David Copperfield.*

MUTANHED, LORD. A visitor at Bath. 'The one with the long hair and the particularly small forehead.'—*The Pickwick Papers.*

NANCY. Member of Fagin's gang of pickpockets and mistress of Bill Sikes, who brutally murdered her. 'The girl's life had been squandered in the streets, and among the most noisome of the stews and dens of London, but there was something of the woman's original nature left in her still.'—*Oliver Twist.*

Rose Maylie, Mr. Brownlow and Nancy

NADGETT. Enquiry agent for the Anglo-Bengalee Company. 'He was mildewed, threadbare, shabby . . . and kept his linen so secret, by buttoning up and wrapping over, that he might have had none—perhaps he hadn't.'—*Martin Chuzzlewit.*

NAMBY. Sheriff's officer. 'He was dressed in a particularly gorgeous manner, with plenty of articles of jewellery about him.'—*The Pickwick Papers.*

NANDY, JOHN EDWARD. Mrs. Plornish's father. 'A poor little reedy, piping old gentleman, like a worn-out bird.'—*Little Dorrit.*

NATIVE, THE. Major Bagstock's man-of-all-work. 'A dark servant of the Major's.'—*Dombey and Son.*

NECKETT. A bailiff. 'With smooth hair upon his head, and not much of it.'—*Bleak House.*

NECKETT, CHARLOTTE ('CHARLEY'). His daughter, aged thirteen, later maid to Esther Summerson. 'A very little girl, childish in figure, but shrewd and older-looking in the face.'—*Bleak House*.

NEWCOME, CLEMENCY. Servant to Doctor Jeddler, later wife to Benjamin Britain. 'To say that she had two left legs and somebody else's arms, and that all four limbs seemed to be out of joint . . . is to offer the mildest outline of the reality.'—*The Battle of Life*.

NICKLEBY, KATE. Sister of Nicholas. 'A slight but very beautiful girl.'—*Nicholas Nickleby*.

NICKLEBY, NICHOLAS. Nephew of Ralph Nickleby; schoolmaster, clerk, actor, and later partner of Cheeryble Brothers. 'There was an emanation from the warm young heart in his look and bearing.'—*Nicholas Nickleby*.

NICKLEBY, RALPH. Uncle of Nicholas, a moneylender. 'He knew himself well, and choosing to imagine that all mankind were cast in the same mould, hated them.'—*Nicholas Nickleby*.

Madeline Bray and Nicholas Nickleby

NICKLEBY, MRS. Mother of Nicholas and Kate. (Portrait, p. 123.) 'A well-meaning woman enough, but weak withal.'—*Nicholas Nickleby*.

NIPPER, SUSAN. Florence Dombey's maid, later wife of Mr. Toots. 'A short brown womanly girl, with a little snub nose and black eyes like jet beads.'—*Dombey and Son.*

Susan Nipper

NOGGS, NEWMAN. Ralph Nickleby's clerk. 'A sallow-faced man in dusty brown . . . the countenance of Newman Noggs in his ordinary moods was a problem which no stretch of ingenuity could solve.'—*Nicholas Nickleby.*

NUBBLES, MRS. Mother of Kit. 'Wait till he's a widder and works like you do, and gets as little, and does as much, and keeps his spirits up the same.'—*The Old Curiosity Shop.*

NUBBLES, JACOB. Brother of Kit. 'A sturdy boy of two or three years old, very wide awake.'—*The Old Curiosity Shop.*

NUBBLES, KIT. Friend of Little Nell. Shop-boy at the Old Curiosity Shop, later employed by Mr. Garland, whose servant, Barbara, he married. 'A shock-headed, shambling, awkward lad with an uncommonly wide mouth, very red cheeks, a turned-up nose, and certainly the most comical expression of face I ever saw.'—*The Old Curiosity Shop.*

NUPKINS, GEORGE. Mayor of Ipswich. 'As grand a personage as the fastest walker would find out between sunrise and sunset.'—*The Pickwick Papers.*

NUPKINS, MRS. 'A majestic female, in a pink gauze turban, and a light brown wig.'—*The Pickwick Papers.*

OBENREIZER, JULES. Wine-merchant's London agent, Swiss-born. 'When colour would have come into another cheek, a hardly discernible beat would come into his, as if the machinery for bringing up the ardent blood were there, but the machinery were dry.'—*No Thoroughfare.*

OBENREIZER, MARGUERITE. Niece of Obenreizer, a Swiss girl, later wife of George Vendale. 'An unusual quantity of fair bright hair, very prettily braided ... her face might have been a shade ... rounder than the average English face.'—*No Thoroughfare.*

OMER, MR. Undertaker, of Yarmouth. 'A fat, short-winded, merry-looking little old man.'—*David Copperfield.*

OMER, MINNIE. His daughter, later wife of Joram. 'A pretty woman at the back of the shop.'—*David Copperfield.*

PANCKS, MR. Factor to Mr. Casby. 'A quick and eager short dark man ... he was in a perspiration, and snorted, and sniffed, and puffed, and blew.'—*Little Dorrit.*

PANKEY, MISS. Boarder at Mrs. Pipchin's. 'A mild little blue-eyed morsel of a child, who was shampooed every morning, and seemed in danger of being rubbed away altogether.'—*Dombey and Son.*

PARAGON, MARY ANNE. The first servant of David and Dora Copperfield. 'Our treasure was warranted sober and honest. I am therefore willing to believe that she was in a fit when we found her under the boiler.'—*David Copperfield.*

PARDIGGLE, MRS. A philanthropic lady, mother of the Pardiggle Boys. 'A formidable style of lady, with spectacles, a prominent nose, and a loud voice, who had the effect of wanting a great deal of room.'—*Bleak House.*

PARDIGGLE BOYS, THE. Alfred, Egbert, Felix, Francis and Oswald. 'Alfred, my youngest (five), has voluntarily enrolled himself in the Infant Bands of Joy, and is pledged never through life to use tobacco in any form. My young family are not frivolous.'—*Bleak House.*

PEAK. Sir John Chester's servant. 'He sank under a contagious disorder, very prevalent at that time, and vulgarly termed the jail fever.'—*Barnaby Rudge*.

PECKSNIFF, CHARITY ('CHERRY'). Elder daughter of Mr. Pecksniff. (Portrait, p. 131.) 'Miss Pecksniff's nose was always red at breakfast-time . . . it wore . . . a scraped and frosty look, as if it had been rasped.'—*Martin Chuzzlewit*.

PECKSNIFF, MERCY ('MERRY'). Younger daughter of Mr. Pecksniff, later wife to Jonas Chuzzlewit. (Portrait, p. 131.) 'She was too fresh and guileless and too full of childlike vivacity—to wear combs in her hair.' 'She laughs so. There's no talking to her.'—*Martin Chuzzlewit*.

PECKSNIFF, SETH. Architect, of Salisbury. 'He was a most exemplary man; fuller of virtuous precept than a copy-book; some people likened him to a direction post, which is always telling the way to a place and never goes there.'—*Martin Chuzzlewit*.

Seth Pecksniff

PEECHER, MISS. School-mistress at Bradley Headstone's school. 'Small, shining, neat, methodical and buxom . . . cherry-cheeked and tuneful of voice; a little pin-cushion; a little housewife . . . '—*Our Mutual Friend*.

PEEPY. Youngest child of Mrs. Jellyby. 'One of the dirtiest little unfortunates I ever saw.'—*Bleak House*.

PEERYBINGLE, JOHN. Carrier. (Portrait, p. 160.) 'This John, so heavy, but so light of spirit; so rough upon the surface, but so gentle at the core.'—*The Cricket on the Hearth*.

PEERYBINGLE, MRS. ('DOT'). Wife of John. (Portrait, p. 160.) 'It was pleasant to see Dot, with her little figure, and her baby in her arms.'—*The Cricket on the Hearth*.

PEGGOTTY, CLARA. Sister of Daniel, later wife to Barkis. 'There was a red velvet footstool in the best parlour. The groundwork of that stool and Peggotty's complexion appeared to me to be one and the same thing.'—*David Copperfield*.

PEGGOTTY, DANIEL. A Yarmouth fisherman. (Portrait, p. 158.) 'A hairy man with a very good-natured face.' —*David Copperfield*.

PEGGOTTY, HAM. Nephew to Daniel, and fiancé of Little Em'ly. 'He was now a huge strong fellow of six feet high, broad in proportion . . . but with a simpering boy's face and curly light hair.'—*David Copperfield*.

PEGLER, MRS. Name assumed by Bounderby's mother. 'An old woman, tall and shapely still, though withered by time.'—*Hard Times*.

PELL, SOLOMON. Insolvent court-attorney. 'A fat, flabby, pale man . . . his nose all on one side, as if Nature, indignant with the propensities she observed in him in his birth, had given it an angry tweak.'—*The Pickwick Papers*.

PEPS, DR. PARKER. Mrs. Dombey's lying-in physician. 'A man of immense reputation for assisting at the increase of great families.'—*Dombey and Son*.

PERCH. Messenger at Dombey and Son's counting-house. 'Whose place was on a little bracket like a time-piece.' —*Dombey and Son*.

PERKER, MR. Solicitor to Mr. Wardle and Mr. Pickwick. 'A little high-dried man, with a dark squeezed-up face, and small restless black eyes . . . his boots were as shiny as his eyes.'—*The Pickwick Papers*.

PETOWKER, MISS HENRIETTA. Of Theatre Royal, Drury Lane, later wife of Mr. Lillyvick. 'Being able to sing and recite in a manner that brought the tears into Mrs. Kenwigs' eyes.'—*Nicholas Nickleby*.

PHUNKY, MR. Junior counsel for Mr. Pickwick. 'Although an infant barrister, he was a full-grown man.'—*The Pickwick Papers*.

PICKWICK, SAMUEL. Founder and general chairman of the Pickwick Club. 'To those who knew that the gigantic brain of Pickwick was working beneath that forehead, and that the beaming eyes of Pickwick were twinkling behind those glasses, the sight was indeed an interesting one.'—*The Pickwick Papers*.

Samuel Pickwick

PINCH, TOM. Assistant to Mr. Pecksniff. 'He was perhaps about thirty, but he might have been almost any age between sixteen and sixty, being one of those strange creatures who never decline into an ancient appearance, but look their oldest when they are very young, and get it over at once.'—*Martin Chuzzlewit*.

Tom Pinch

PINCH, RUTH. Sister of Tom, later wife of John Westlock. 'There was something of her brother, much of him indeed, in a certain gentleness of manner, and in her look of timid trustfulness.'—*Martin Chuzzlewit*.

PIPCHIN, MRS. Keeper of a children's boarding-house at Brighton. (Portrait, p. 136.) 'A marvellous ill-favoured, ill-conditioned old lady, of a stooping figure, with a mottled face like bad marble.'—*Dombey and Son*.

PIPKIN, NATHANIEL. Hero of Sam Weller's tale of 'The Parish Clerk'. 'A harmless, inoffensive, good-natured being; with a turned-up nose; and rather turned-in legs . . .'—*The Pickwick Papers*.

PIRRIP, PHILIP ('PIP'). An orphan, brother of Mrs. Joe Gargery. 'A good fellow, with impetuosity and hesitation, boldness and diffidence, action and dreaming curiously mixed in him.'—*Great Expectations*.

PLORNISH. Plasterer, of Bleeding Heart Yard. 'A willing, working, soft-hearted, not hard-headed fellow.'—*Little Dorrit*.

PLORNISH, MRS. His wife. 'So dragged at, by poverty and the children together, that their united forces had already dragged her face into wrinkles.'—*Little Dorrit*.

PLUCK. Toady of Sir Mulberry Hawk. 'A gentleman with a flushed face and a flash air.'—*Nicholas Nickleby*.

PLUMMER, CALEB. A poor toy-maker employed by Gruff and Tackleton. 'Never had he, when his heart was heaviest, forgotten the light tread that was to render hers so cheerful and courageous.'—*The Cricket on the Hearth*.

Caleb Plummer

PLUMMER, BERTHA. His blind daughter. 'Happy blind girl . . . turning up her radiant face.'—*The Cricket on the Hearth*.

PLUMMER, EDWARD. Son of Caleb and later married to May Fielding. 'The sunburnt sailor-fellow, with his dark streaming hair.'—*The Cricket on the Hearth*.

POCKET, MATTHEW. Cousin of Miss Havisham; a tutor. 'When he had the happiness of marrying Mrs. Pocket . . . had impaired his prospects, and taken up the calling of a Grinder.'—*Great Expectations*.

POCKET, MRS. BELINDA. 'She had grown up highly ornamental but perfectly helpless and useless . . . '—*Great Expectations*.

POCKET, MISS GEORGINA. Cousin of Matthew. 'An indigestive single woman who called her rigidity religion, and her liver love.'—*Great Expectations*.

POCKET, HERBERT. Pip's friend, later husband of Clara Barley. 'There was something wonderfully hopeful about his general air, and something that at the same time whispered to me that he would never be very successful or rich.'—*Great Expectations*.

PODSNAP, GEORGIANA. Daughter of Mr. and Mrs. John Podsnap. Usually referred to as 'the young person'. 'She was but an undersized damsel, with high shoulders, low spirits, chilled elbows, and a rasped surface of nose, who seemed to take occasional frosty peeps out of childhood into womanhood.'—*Our Mutual Friend*.

PODSNAP, MR. JOHN. Of the Marine Insurance. 'A too-smiling large man, with a fatal freshness on him.'—*Our Mutual Friend*.

PODSNAP, MRS. 'Fine woman for Professor Owen, quantity of bone, neck and nostrils like a rocking-horse; hard features; majestic head-dress.'—*Our Mutual Friend*.

POGRAM, THE HON. ELIJAH. Fellow-traveller of Martin Chuzzlewit in America. 'His complexion, naturally muddy, was rendered muddier by too strict an economy of soap and water.'—*Martin Chuzzlewit*.

POTT, MR. Editor of the *Eatanswill Gazette*. 'A face in which solemn importance was blended with a look of unfathomable profundity.'—*The Pickwick Papers*.

POTT, MRS. His wife. 'Who would have looked very like Apollo if she hadn't had a gown on.'—*The Pickwick Papers*.

POTTERSON, MISS ABBEY. Proprietor and manager of the 'Six Jolly Fellowship Porters'. ' . . . severe of countenance, and had more the air of a schoolmistress.' —*Our Mutual Friend*.

POTTERSON, JOB. Miss Abbey's brother, a ship's steward. 'There's an air of reliability about him in case you wanted a basin, which points out the steward.'—*Our Mutual Friend*.

Abbey Potterson

PRICE, MATILDA. Friend of Fanny Squeers, afterwards wife of John Browdie. 'She was pretty, and a coquette, too, in her small way.'—*Nicholas Nickleby*.

PRIG, MRS. BETSEY. A nurse, friend of Mrs. Gamp. (Portrait, p. 42.) 'Of the Gamp build, but not so fat; and her voice was deeper and more like a man's; she had also a beard.'—*Martin Chuzzlewit.*

PROSS, MISS. Companion and friend of Lucie Manette. 'A wild-looking woman . . . all of a red colour . . . dressed in some extraordinary tight-fitting fashion.'—*A Tale of Two Cities.*

'PUFFER, PRINCESS.' Keeper of a London opium den. 'Ah, my poor nerves! I got Heavens hard drunk for sixteen year afore I took to this; but this don't hurt me, not to speak of.'—*Edwin Drood.*

Miss Pross

PUMBLECHOOK. A corn chandler, uncle of Joe Gargery. 'He looked as if he had just been all but choked, and had that moment come to.'—*Great Expectations.*

PYKE, MR. Toady of Sir Mulberry Hawk. 'A sharp-faced gentleman.'—*Nicholas Nickleby.*

QUALE, MR. Admirer of Caddy Jellyby. 'A loquacious young man . . . with large shining knobs for temples.'—*Bleak House.*

QUILP, DANIEL. A dwarf, rent-collector, money-lender, and smuggler. 'The creature appeared quite horrible with his monstrous head and little body.'—*The Old Curiosity Shop.*

Daniel Quilp

QUILP, MRS. 'A pretty, little mild-spoken blue-eyed woman; who, having allied herself in wedlock to the dwarf . . . performed a sound practical penance for her folly every day of her life.'—*The Old Curiosity Shop*.

RACHAEL. Factory worker at Coketown. 'It was not a face in its first bloom.'—*Hard Times*.

Rachael

RACHAEL, MRS. Nurse of Esther Summerson in childhood, later wife to Mr. Chadband. 'Another very good woman but austere to me.'—*Bleak House*.

RADDLE, MRS. Bob Sawyer's landlady, sister of Mrs. Cluppins. 'A little fierce woman.'—*The Pickwick Papers*.

REDLAW, MR. The Haunted Man. Chemist-lecturer beset by unhappy memories. 'Who could have seen his hollow cheek, his sunken, brilliant eye; his black-attired figure . . . but might have said he looked like a haunted man?' —*The Haunted Man*.

RIAH, MR. A Jew, who conducted the business of Pubsey and Co. 'A venerable man, bald and shining at the top of his head, and with long grey hair flowing down at its sides.'—*Our Mutual Friend*.

RICHARD. A blacksmith, Meg Veck's sweetheart. 'With eyes that sparkled like the red-hot droppings from a furnace fire, black hair that curled about his swarthy temples rarely, and a smile . . . that bore out Meg's eulogium on his style of conversation.'—*The Chimes*.

RIDERHOOD, ROGER ('ROGUE'). First partner, then enemy to Gaffer Hexam. 'An ill-looking visitor with a squinting leer.'—*Our Mutual Friend*.

RIDERHOOD, MISS PLEASANT. Daughter of Roger Riderhood, later wife of Mr. Venus. 'Her hair was a ragged knot constantly coming down behind.'—*Our Mutual Friend*.

RIGAUD. Alias Blandois, alias Lagnier. Adventurer and blackmailer. 'He had a certain air of being a handsome man, which he was not; and a certain air of being a well-bred man, which he was not.'—*Little Dorrit*.

ROKESMITH, JOHN. *See* HARMON, JOHN—*Our Mutual Friend*.

Rigaud

ROSA. Mrs. Rouncewell's maid, later wife of Walter Rouncewell. 'A dark-eyed, dark-haired, shy village beauty.' —*Bleak House*.

ROUNCEWELL, MRS. Housekeeper to Sir Leicester Dedlock at Chesney Wold. 'If her stays should turn out when she dies to have been a broad, old-fashioned, family firegrate, nobody who knows her would have cause to be surprised.'—*Bleak House*.

ROUNCEWELL, MR. Her elder son, an ironmaster. 'He is a responsible-looking gentleman, dressed in black.' —*Bleak House*.

ROUNCEWELL, GEORGE. Younger son of Mrs. Rouncewell. Keeper of a shooting-gallery. 'His sinewy and powerful hands, as sunburnt as his face, have evidently been used to a pretty rough life.'—*Bleak House*.

Rouncewell, Watt. Son of Mr. Rouncewell the iron-master. 'You are a fine fellow. You are like your poor Uncle George.'—*Bleak House*.

Rudge, Barnaby. A youth of retarded intellect. (Portrait, p. 129.) 'His hair . . . hanging in disorder about his face and shoulders, gave to his restless looks an expression quite unearthly.'—*Barnaby Rudge*.

Rudge, Mrs. Mary. Barnaby's mother. 'Where, in his face, there was wildness and vacancy, in hers there was the quiet composure of long effort and patient resignation.' —*Barnaby Rudge*.

Rudge, Mr. Father of Barnaby, formerly steward to Reuben Haredale, then his murderer. 'The hard features of a man of sixty or thereabouts . . . the naturally harsh expression of which was not improved by a dark handker-chief.'—*Barnaby Rudge*.

Rugg, Mr. General agent, accountant, debt-collector, and Mr. Panck's landlord. 'A round white visage, as if all his blushes had been drawn out of him long ago.'—*Little Dorrit*.

Rugg, Miss Anastasia. 'Her heart severely lacerated, and her feelings mangled, by a middle-aged baker.' —*Little Dorrit*.

St. Evremonde, The Marquis. Uncle of Charles Darnay, an aristocrat. 'With a face like a fine mask; a face of transparent paleness.'—*A Tale of Two Cities*.

Sally, Old. Pauper attendant at Oliver Twist's birth. 'Who was rendered rather misty by an unwonted allow-ance of beer.'—*Oliver Twist*.

SAMPSON, GEORGE. Formerly admirer of Bella Wilfer, later transferred to her sister Lavinia. 'He sat down . . . as if he felt himself full to the throat with affronting sentiments.'—*Our Mutual Friend*.

SANDERS, MRS. Friend of Mrs. Bardell. 'A big, fat, heavy-faced personage.'—*The Pickwick Papers*.

SAPSEA, THOMAS. Auctioneer, and Mayor of Cloisterham. 'Morally satisfied that nothing but he himself has grown since he was a baby.'—*Edwin Drood*.

SAWYER, BOB. A medical student. 'He eschewed gloves, and looked upon the whole something like a dissipated Robinson Crusoe.'—*The Pickwick Papers*.

Bob Sawyer and Sam Weller

SCADDER, ZEPHANIAH. Agent of the Eden Land Corporation. 'Every time he spoke, something was seen to twitch and jerk up in his throat, like the little hammers in a harpsichord.'—*Martin Chuzzlewit*.

SCADGERS, LADY. Mrs. Sparsit's great-aunt. 'With an inordinate appetite for butcher's meat, and a mysterious leg, which had now refused to get out of bed for fourteen years.'—*Hard Times*.

SCOTT, TOM. In charge of Quilp's Wharf. 'An amphibious boy in a canvas suit.'—*The Old Curiosity Shop*.

SCROOGE, EBENEZER. A miser. (Portraits, pp. 157, 158.) Surviving partner of Scrooge and Marley. 'The cold within him froze his old features . . . he carried his own low temperature always about with him; he iced his coffee in the dog days.'—*A Christmas Carol.*

SHARP, MR. First master at Salem House. 'A way of carrying his head on one side, as if it were a little too heavy for him.'—*David Copperfield.*

SHEPHERD, MISS. Boarder at the Misses Nettingall's establishment for young ladies: one of David Copperfield's first loves. 'A little girl, in a spencer, with a round face and curly flaxen hair.'—*David Copperfield.*

SHORT, otherwise Trotters. Real name Harris. Partner with Codlin in the Punch and Judy show. 'A little merry-faced man, with a twinkling eye, and a red nose.'—*The Old Curiosity Shop.*

SIKES, BILL. A housebreaker, member of Fagin's gang and lover of Nancy. 'The kind of legs which . . . always look in an unfinished and incomplete state, without a set of fetters to garnish them.'—*Oliver Twist.*

SINGLE GENTLEMAN, THE. Brother of Little Nell's grandfather, and lodger at the house of Sampson Brass. 'He was a brown-faced sunburnt man, and appeared browner and more sunburnt from having a white night-cap on.'—*The Old Curiosity Shop.*

SKETTLES, SIR BARNET, M.P. Parent of a prospective pupil of Dr. Blimber. 'When he *did* catch the Speaker's eye . . . it was anticipated that he would rather touch up the Radicals.'—*Dombey and Son.*

SKETTLES, MASTER. Prospective pupil of Dr. Blimber.
'Was revenging himself for the studies to come on the
plum cake.'—*Dombey and Son*.

Bill Sikes and Bull's-Eye

Skewton, The Hon. Mrs. ('Cleopatra') Mother of Edith Granger. 'Although the old lady was not young, she was very blooming in the face.'—*Dombey and Son*.

Skiffins, Miss. Afterwards the wife of Mr. Wemmick. 'She seemed to be a good sort of fellow.'—*Great Expectations*.

Skimpole, Harold. An impecunious dilettante. 'He was a little, bright creature, with a rather large head, but a delicate face and a sweet voice, and there was a perfect charm in him.'—*Bleak House*.

Harold Skimpole

Skimpole, Mrs. Harold. 'A delicate, high-nosed invalid.'—*Bleak House*.

Skimpole, The Misses. Arethusa, Laura, and Kitty. 'My Beauty daughter . . . my Sentiment daughter . . . my Comedy daughter . . . we all draw a little, and compose a little, and none of us have any idea of time or money.'—*Bleak House*.

Slammer, Dr. Surgeon to the 97th Regiment. (Portrait, p. 53.) 'The Doctor took snuff with everybody, chatted with everybody, laughed, danced . . . did everything, and was everywhere.'—*The Pickwick Papers*.

Sleary, Mr. Circus proprietor. 'With one fixed eye and one loose eye; a voice . . . like the efforts of a broken old pair of bellows.'—*Hard Times*.

Sleary, Josephine. His daughter, an equestrienne, married to E. W. B. Childers. 'Had made a will at twelve . . . expressive of her dying desire to be drawn to the grave by the two piebald ponies.'—*Hard Times*.

SLIDERSKEW, PEG. Housekeeper to Arthur Gride. 'Palsy stricken and hideously ugly.'—*Nicholas Nickleby.*

SLOPPY. A mangle-turning foundling kept by Betty Higden. 'A very long boy, with a very little head, and an open mouth of disproportionate capacity.'—*Our Mutual Friend.*

SLOWBOY, TILLY. Mrs. Peery-bingle's maid. 'She was of a spare and straight shape . . . her garments appeared to be in constant danger of sliding off those sharp pegs her shoulders.'—*The Cricket on the Hearth.*

Tilly Slowboy

SLUMKEY, THE HON. SAMUEL. Successful Blue candidate in the Eatanswill Election. 'He has patted the babies on the head . . . he has kissed one of 'em . . . he has kissed another . . . he's kissing 'em all!'—*The Pickwick Papers.*

SLURK, MR. Editor of the *Eatanswill Independent.* 'His aspect was pompous and threatening; his manner was peremptory.'—*The Pickwick Papers.*

SLYME, CHEVY. Nephew of old Martin Chuzzlewit. 'This off-shoot of the Chuzzlewit trunk, being lazy, and ill-qualified for any regular pursuit . . .'—*Martin Chuzzlewit.*

SMALLWEED, BART. Junior law clerk, friend of Mr. Guppy. 'A town-made article, of small stature and weazen features.'—*Bleak House.*

SMALLWEED, MR., his paralysed grandfather. 'Everything . . . ever put away in his mind was a grub at first, and is a grub at last; in all his life he has never bred a single butterfly.'—*Bleak House.*

SMALLWEED, MRS. His wife, sister of Krook. 'With such infantine graces as a total want of observation, memory, understanding, and interest'.—*Bleak House.*

SMALLWEED, JUDY. Twin sister of Bart. 'Judy never owned a doll, never heard of Cinderella, never played at any game. One might infer from Judy's appearance that her business lay with the thorns rather than the flowers.'—*Bleak House.*

Judy Smallweed

SMANGLE, MR. Prisoner for debt, in the Fleet. 'There was a rakish vagabond smartness, and a kind of boastful rascality about the whole man, that was worth a mine of gold.'—*The Pickwick Papers.*

SMART, TOM. A commercial traveller, hero of 'The Bagman's Story'. 'Of the great house of Bilson and Slum, Cateaton Street, City.'—*The Pickwick Papers.*

SMAUKER, MR. A footman at Bath. 'The gentleman who had the pleasure of meeting Mr. Weller at the house of their mutual acquaintance Mr. Bantam.'—*The Pickwick Papers.*

SMIKE. Natural son of Ralph Nickleby, a pupil at Dotheboys Hall, later a strolling player. 'Although he could not have been less than eighteen or nineteen years old, and was tall for that age, he wore a skeleton suit, such as is usually put upon very little boys.'—*Nicholas Nickleby*.

SMORLTORK, COUNT. Guest at Mrs. Leo Hunter's *fête champêtre*. 'A well-whiskered individual in a foreign uniform.'—*The Pickwick Papers*.

SNAGSBY, MR. A law stationer. 'A mild, bald, timid man . . . he tends to meekness and obesity.'—*Bleak House*.

SNAGSBY, MRS. 'With a sharp nose, like a sharp autumn evening, inclined to be frosty towards the end.'—*Bleak House*.

SNAWLEY. Stepfather of two boys at Dotheboys Hall. 'A sleek, flat-nosed man, bearing . . . an expression of much mortification and sanctity.'—*Nicholas Nickleby*.

SNEVELLICCI, MISS. Actress in Mr. Crummles' company. 'Could do anything, from a medley dance to Lady Macbeth, and also always played some part in blue silk knee-smalls at her benefit.'—*Nicholas Nickleby*.

SNEVELLICCI, MR. Her father, an actor in Mr. Crummles' company. 'Was always selected, in virtue of his figure, to play the military visitors, and the speechless noblemen.'—*Nicholas Nickleby*.

SNEVELLICCI, MRS. 'Who was still a dancer, with a neat little figure . . . and who now sat, as she danced . . . in the background.'—*Nicholas Nickleby*.

SNITCHEY. A lawyer, partner with Craggs. 'I don't stand up for life in general, its full of folly—full of something worse—professions of trust, and confidence, and unselfishness, and all that.'—*The Battle of Life*.

SNODGRASS, AUGUSTUS. Member of the Pickwick Club. 'The poetic Snodgrass, poetically enveloped in a mysterious blue cloak with a canine skin collar.'—*The Pickwick Papers*.

SNUBBIN, SERJEANT. Counsel for Mr. Pickwick. 'A lantern-faced, sallow-complexioned man . . . far too much occupied with his professional pursuits to take any great heed or regard of his personal comforts.'—*The Pickwick Papers*.

SNUPHANUPH, LADY. A visitor at Bath. '"The fat old lady?" enquired Mr. Pickwick, innocently. "Hush, my dear sir, nobody's fat or old in Bath".'—*The Pickwick Papers*.

SOWERBERRY, MR. An undertaker, to whom Oliver was apprenticed. 'His features were not naturally intended to wear a smiling aspect, but he was in general rather given to professional jocosity.'—*Oliver Twist*.

SOWERBERRY, MRS. 'With a vixenish countenance.' —*Oliver Twist*.

SPARKLER, EDMUND. Mrs. Merdle's son by her first marriage. 'Of a chuckle-headed, high-shouldered make, with a general appearance of being not so much a young man as a swelled boy.'—*Little Dorrit*.

SPARSIT, MRS. Mr. Bounderby's housekeeper. 'Had not only seen different days, but was highly connected.' —*Hard Times*.

SPENLOW, MR. FRANCIS. A proctor, partner of Spenlow and Jorkins. 'He was got up with such care, and was so stiff, that he could hardly bend himself.'—*David Copperfield*.

SPENLOW, DORA. His daughter, afterwards first wife of David Copperfield.
'She had the most delightful little voice
... the pleasantest and most fascinating
little ways that ever led a lost youth into
hopeless slavery.'—*David Copperfield*.

Dora Spenlow

SPENLOW, THE MISSES LAVINIA AND
CLARISSA. Dora's maiden aunts. 'Two
dry little elderly ladies ... they were not unlike birds
altogether, having a ... little short spruce way of adjusting
themselves, like canaries.'—*David Copperfield*.

SPIKER, MRS. HENRY. Introduced to David Copperfield
at dinner. 'A very awful lady in a black velvet dress, and a
great black velvet hat ... looking like a near relation of
Hamlet's—say his aunt.'—*David Copperfield*.

SPOTTLETOE, MR. Relative of old Martin Chuzzlewit.
'Who was so bald, and had such big whiskers, that he
seemed to have stopped his hair, by the sudden application
of some powerful remedy, in the very act of falling off his
head, and to have fastened it irrevocably on his face.'
—*Martin Chuzzlewit*.

SPOTTLETOE, MRS. 'Much
too slim for her years, and of
a poetical constitution.'—
Martin Chuzzlewit.

SQUEERS, MR. WACK-
FORD. Proprietor of Dotheboys Hall. 'He had but one
eye, and the popular preju-
dice runs in favour of two
... The blank side of his
face was much wrinkled and

Wackford Squeers and Pupil

puckered up, which gave him a very sinister appearance, especially when he smiled.'—*Nicholas Nickleby.*

SQUEERS, MRS. WACKFORD. 'Of a large raw-boned figure . . . she had also a dirty night-cap on, relieved by a yellow cotton handkerchief.'—*Nicholas Nickleby.*

SQUEERS, MISS FANNY. Their daughter. 'She was not tall like her mother, but short like her father; from the former she inherited a voice of harsh quality; from the latter a remarkable expression of the right eye, something akin to having none at all.'—*Nicholas Nickleby.*

SQUEERS, MASTER WACKFORD. Her brother. 'His chief amusement was to tread upon the other boys' toes in his new boots.'—*Nicholas Nickleby.*

SQUOD, PHIL. Attendant at Mr. George's shooting-gallery. 'A little man, with a face all crushed together.' —*Bleak House.*

STAGG. A blind man, keeper of the headquarters of the Prentice Knights. 'He wore an old tie wig, as bare and frowzy as a stunted hearth broom.'—*Barnaby Rudge.*

STARELEIGH, MR. JUSTICE. Judge at the Bardell *v.* Pickwick trial. 'A most particularly short man, and so fat that he seemed all face and waistcoat.'—*The Pickwick Papers.*

STEERFORTH, JAMES. School-fellow and later friend of David Copperfield, seducer of Little Em'ly. ' . . . this boy, who was reputed to be a great scholar, and was very good-looking, and at least half-a-dozen years my senior.'—*David Copperfield.*

*Miss Mowcher and
James Steerforth*

STEERFORTH, MRS. His mother. 'With a proud carriage and a handsome face.'—*David Copperfield*.

STIGGINS, MR. A lay preacher, friend of Mrs. Tony Weller. 'A prim-faced, red-nosed man, with a long thin countenance, and a semi-rattlesnake sort of eye.'—*The Pickwick Papers*.

STRONG, DOCTOR. Master of the school at Canterbury attended by David Copperfield. 'He was the kindest of men; with a simple faith in him that might have touched the stone hearts of the very urns upon the wall.'—*David Copperfield*.

STRONG, MRS. ANNIE. 'He had married for love, for she had not a sixpence, and had a world of poor relations.' —*David Copperfield*.

STRYVER, MR. London barrister defending Darnay. 'Stout, loud, red, bluff, and free from any drawback of delicacy.'—*A Tale of Two Cities*.

SUMMERSON, ESTHER. Natural daughter of Lady Dedlock and Captain Hawdon, later the wife of Allan Woodcourt.' You're a dear, good, wise, quiet, blessed girl.' —*Bleak House*.

SWEEDLEPIPE, PAUL. Barber and bird-fancier. 'With a clammy cold right hand, from which even rabbits and birds could not remove the smell of shaving-soap.'—*Martin Chuzzlewit*.

'SWEET WILLIAM.' A travelling showman, cardsharper and conjurer. 'Who had rather deranged the natural expression of his countenance by putting small leaden lozenges into his eyes, and bringing them out by his mouth.'—*The Old Curiosity Shop*.

SWIDGER, GEORGE. Feckless brother of William Swidger, brought low by gambling. '...a man who should have been in the vigour of his life, but on whom it was not likely the sun would ever shine again.'—*The Haunted Man.*

SWIDGER, MILLY. Wife of William Swidger and Matron of the Institution where Redlaw lectured. 'A sort of mother to all the young gentlemen that come up from a variety of parts.'—*The Haunted Man.*

SWIDGER, PHILIP. Father of William and George Swidger. 'Why, there's my father, sir, superannuated Keeper and Custodian of this Institution.'—*The Haunted Man.*

SWIDGER, WILLIAM. Husband of Milly and Keeper of the Institution. 'A fresh-coloured busy man.'—*The Haunted Man.*

SWIVELLER, RICHARD. Clerk to Sampson Brass, friend of Fred Trent, and later husband of 'The Marchioness'. 'His attire was not ...remarkable for the nicest arrangement, but was in a state of disorder which strongly induced the idea that he had gone to bed in it.'—*The Old Curiosity Shop.*

Richard Swiveller

TACKLETON. A toy merchant. 'A man whose vocation had been quite misunderstood by his Parents and Guardians.'—*The Cricket on the Hearth.*

TADGER, BROTHER. Member of the Brick Lane Branch of the United Grand Junction Ebenezer Temperance Association. 'A little emphatic man, with a bald head and drab shorts.'—*The Pickwick Papers.*

TAMAROO. An old woman working at Todgers' boarding-house. 'She . . . always wore . . . bandages on her wrists, which appeared to be afflicted with an everlasting sprain . . . and she waited at table in a bonnet.'—*Martin Chuzzlewit.*

TAPLEY, MARK. Ostler at the Blue Dragon, later Martin Chuzzlewit's servant and husband of Mrs. Lupin. (Portrait, p. 132.) 'Lord bless you, sir . . . I don't believe there ever was a man as could come out so strong under circumstances that would make other men miserable, as I could if I could only get a chance.'—*Martin Chuzzlewit.*

TAPPERTIT, SIMON. Apprentice of Gabriel Varden, and Gordon Rioter. 'An old fashioned, thin-faced, sleek-haired, sharp-nosed, small-eyed little fellow . . . he also had some majestic shadow ideas . . . concerning the power of his eye.'—*Barnaby Rudge.*

Simon Tappertit

TARTAR, LIEUTENANT, R.N. Neville Landless's neighbour in Staple Inn. 'A handsome gentleman . . . broad temples, bright blue eyes, clustering brown hair, and laughing teeth.'—*Edwin Drood.*

TATTYCORAM, otherwise Harriet Beadle. A foundling brought up by the Meagles as maid and companion to Pet. 'A handsome girl, with lustrous dark hair and eyes, and very neatly dressed.'—*Little Dorrit.*

TETTERBY, ADOLPHUS. Impoverished newsvendor of Jerusalem Buildings. (Portrait, p. 165.) 'A small man sat in a small parlour, partitioned off from a small shop by a small screen pasted all over with small scraps of newspapers.' —*The Haunted Man.*

TETTERBY, ADOLPHUS, JUNIOR. Son of Mr. Tetterby, a newsboy. 'Employed . . . to vend newspapers at a railway station, where his chubby little person, like a shabbily disguised cupid, and his shrill little voice . . . were as well known as the hoarse panting of the locomotives.'—*The Haunted Man.*

TETTERBY, JOHNNY. Brother of Adolphus Junior. (Portrait, p. 165.) 'Another little boy—the biggest there but still little—was tottering to and fro, bent on one side . . . by the weight of a large baby.'—*The Haunted Man.*

TETTERBY, MRS. ADOLPHUS, called by her husband 'my little woman'. 'She was rather remarkable for being robust and portly, but considered with reference to her husband, her dimensions became magnificent.'—*The Haunted Man.*

TETTERBY, SALLY. The Tetterbys' baby. 'It was a very Moloch of a baby, on whose insatiate altar the whole existence of this particular young brother was offered up a daily sacrifice.'—*The Haunted Man.*

TIGG, MONTAGUE (TIGG MONTAGUE). An adventurer, murdered by Jonas Chuzzlewit. 'Very dirty, and very jaunty, very bold, and very mean; very swaggering, and very slinking; very much like a man who might have been something better, and unspeakingly like a man who deserved to be something worse.' —*Martin Chuzzlewit.*

TIMBERRY, SNITTLE. Actor in Mr. Crummles' company. 'In the most approved attitude, with one hand in the breast of his waistcoat, and the other on the nearest snuffbox.'—*Nicholas Nickleby.*

Tigg Montague

TINY TIM. Youngest child of Bob Cratchit; a cripple. 'He bore a little crutch, and had his limbs supported by an iron frame . . . as good as gold . . . somehow he gets thoughtful, sitting by himself so much.'—*A Christmas Carol.*

TISHER, MRS. Companion and assistant of Miss Twinkleton. 'A deferential widow, with a weak back, a chronic sigh, and a suppressed voice.'—*Edwin Drood.*

TODGERS, MRS. Proprietor of the Commercial Boarding-House in London. 'Rather a bony and hard-featured lady, with a row of curls in front of her head, shaped like little barrels of beer, and on the top of it something made of net—you couldn't call it a cap exactly—which looked like a black cobweb.'—*Martin Chuzzlewit.*

TOODLE, MRS. POLLY. Wife of an engine-driver, wet nurse to Paul Dombey. 'A plump, rosy-cheeked, wholesome, apple-faced young woman.'—*Dombey and Son.*

TOODLE, ROBIN. Polly Toodle's eldest son. Known as Rob the Grinder and also 'Biler'. Later a spy for Carker, and Miss Tox's page. 'A strong-built lad of fifteen, with a round red face, a round sleek head . . . who, to carry out the general rotundity of his appearance, had a round hat in his hand.'—*Dombey and Son.*

TOOTS, MR. A pupil at Dr. Blimber's, friend of Paul Dombey, later husband of Susan Nipper. 'With a swollen nose and an excessively large head . . . suddenly left off blowing one day, and remained in the establishment a mere stalk.'—*Dombey and Son.*

TOPE, MR. Verger at Cloisterham Cathedral. 'Accustomed to be high with excursion parties.'—*Edwin Drood.*

TOX, MISS LUCRETIA. Friend of Mrs. Chick, and admirer of Mr. Dombey. 'A long lean figure, wearing such a faded air, that she seemed not to have been made in what linen-drapers call fast colours originally, and to have, by little and little, washed out.' —*Dombey and Son.*

Miss Lucretia Tox

TRABB. A master tailor. 'He was a prosperous old bachelor.'—*Great Expectations.*

TRABB'S BOY. 'The most audacious boy in all that country-side.'—*Great Expectations.*

TRADDLES, THOMAS. Fellow-pupil at Salem House of David Copperfield, later a barrister. 'In a tight sky-blue suit that made his arms and legs like German sausages or roly-poly puddings, he was the merriest and most miserable of all the boys.'—*David Copperfield.*

Thomas Traddles

TRENT, MR. Grandfather of 'Little Nell', proprietor of The Old Curiosity Shop. 'The haggard aspect of the little old man was wonderfully suited to the place; he might have groped among old churches, and tombs . . . and gathered all the spoils with his own hands.'—*The Old Curiosity Shop.*

TRENT, FRED. Brother of Little Nell. 'Having . . . a dissipated, insolent air which repelled one.'—*The Old Curiosity Shop.*

TRENT, NELL ('LITTLE NELL'). Grand-daughter of old Trent, and companion in his wanderings; died young. 'A pretty little girl . . . her very small and delicate frame imparted a peculiar youthfulness to her appearance.'—*The Old Curiosity Shop.*

Nell Trent and her Grandfather

TROTTER, JOB. Servant and accomplice of Jingle. 'A young fellow in mulberry-coloured livery.'—*The Pickwick Papers.*

TROTWOOD, MISS BETSEY. Great-
aunt of David Copperfield, and later
his guardian. 'A tall, hard-featured
lady, but by no means ill-looking . . .
her features were rather handsome
than otherwise, though unbending
and austere . . . she had a very quick,
bright eye.'—*David Copperfield*.

*Miss Betsey
Trotwood*

TRUNDLE, MR. Bridegroom of
Isabella Wardle. 'A young gentleman
apparently enamoured of one of the young ladies in scarfs
and feathers'.—*The Pickwick Papers*.

TUGBY. Porter at Sir Joseph Bowley's. 'Such a Porter!
. . . ' 'His voice . . . was a long way off, and hidden under a
load of meat.'—*The Chimes*.

TULKINGHORN. Family lawyer of Sir Leicester Dedlock.
'An Oyster of the old school, whom nobody can open.'
—*Bleak House*.

TUNGAY. Porter at Salem House. 'A bull-neck, a wooden
leg, overhanging temples . . . considered the whole establishment, masters and boys, as his natural enemies.'
—*David Copperfield*.

TUPMAN, TRACY. Member of the Pickwick Club. 'Time
and feeding had expanded that once romantic form; the
black silk waistcoat had become more and more
developed.'—*The Pickwick Papers*.

TURVEYDROP, PRINCE. A dancing master, husband of
Caddy Jellyby. 'A little, blue-eyed, fair man . . . he had a
little innocent feminine manner.'—*Bleak House*.

TURVEYDROP, MR. Prince's father. 'He was not like youth, he was not like age; he was not like anything in the world but a model of Deportment.'—*Bleak House.*

TWEMLOW, MELVIN. Regular guest of the Veneerings and cousin of Lord Snigsworth. 'Grey, dry, polite, susceptible to east wind. First-gentleman-in-Europe collar and cravat, cheeks drawn as if he had made a great effort to retire into himself, some years ago, and had got so far and never got any further.'—*Our Mutual Friend.*

Mr. Turveydrop

TWINKLETON, MISS. Principal of the Nuns' House Ladies' Seminary, Cloisterham. 'Every night at the same hour does Miss Twinkleton smarten up her curls a little, brighten up her eyes a little, and become a sprightlier Miss Twinkleton than the young ladies have ever seen.'—*Edwin Drood.*

TWIST, OLIVER. A parish foundling, the natural son of Edwin Leeford and Agnes Fleming. 'A pale, thin child, somewhat diminutive in stature and decidedly small in circumference. But Nature . . . had implanted a good sturdy spirit in Oliver's breast.'—*Oliver Twist.*

VARDEN, GABRIEL. A locksmith. 'A round, red-faced, sturdy yeoman, with a double chin and a voice husky with good living, good sleeping, good humour, and good health.'—*Barnaby Rudge.*

VARDEN, MRS. 'It generally happened that, when other people were merry, Mrs. Varden was dull; and that when other people were dull, Mrs. Varden was disposed to be amazingly cheerful.'—*Barnaby Rudge*.

VARDEN, DOLLY. Daughter of Gabriel. (Portrait, p. 128.) Later the wife of Joe Willet. 'A roguish face . . . lighted up by the loveliest pair of sparkling eyes that ever locksmith looked upon . . . the very impersonation of good humour and blooming beauty.'—*Barnaby Rudge*.

VECK, TOBY ('TROTTY'). A London ticket-porter. (Portrait, p. 162.) 'A weak, small, spare old man, he was a very Hercules, this Toby, in his good intentions.'—*The Chimes*.

VECK, MEG. Toby Veck's daughter, later the wife of Richard. 'Eyes that were beautiful and true, and beaming with Hope—with Hope so young and fresh.'—*The Chimes*.

VENDALE, GEORGE. Partner in the firm of Wilding and Co., later discovered to be the real Walter Wilding; married Marguerite Obenreizer. 'A brown-cheeked handsome fellow . . . with a quick determined eye and an impulsive manner.'—*No Thoroughfare*.

VENEERING, HAMILTON, M.P. Partner in the firm of Chicksey, Veneering and Stobbles. 'Mr. and Mrs. Veneering were bran-new people in a bran-new house in a bran-new quarter of London.'—*Our Mutual Friend*.

VENGEANCE, THE. Woman Revolutionary, associate of Madame Defarge. 'The short, rather plump, wife of a starved grocer.'—*A Tale of Two Cities*.

VENUS, MR. Taxidermist and articulator of bones. 'If you was brought here loose in a bag, to be articulated, I'd name your smallest bones blindfold . . . and I'd sort 'em all, and sort your wertebrae, in a manner that would equally surprise and charm you.'—*Our Mutual Friend*.

VERISOPHT, LORD FREDERICK. Business acquaintance of Ralph Nickleby, dupe of Sir Mulberry Hawk, and admirer of Kate Nickleby; killed in a duel. 'The unfortunate young Lord, who, weak and silly as he was, appeared by far the least vicious of the party.'—*Nicholas Nickleby*.

VHOLES, MR. Richard Carstone's Chancery solicitor. 'There was nothing so remarkable in him as a lifeless manner.'—*Bleak House*.

VOIGT, MAÎTRE. A notary in Neuchâtel. 'A rosy, hearty, handsome old man.'—*No Thoroughfare*.

Mr. Vholes

WACKLES, MISS SOPHY. Admired by Dick Swiveller; later wife of Mr. Cheggs. 'A fresh, good-humoured, buxom girl of twenty.'—*The Old Curiosity Shop*.

WADE, MISS. Fellow-traveller of the Meagles family. 'A handsome young Englishwoman, travelling quite alone, who had a proud, observant face.'—*Little Dorrit*.

WARDEN, MICHAEL. Client of Snitchey and Craggs. In love with Marion Jeddler, ultimately married to her. 'There was something naturally graceful and pleasant in the very carelessness of his air.'—*The Battle of Life*.

WARDLE, MR., of Manor Farm, Dingley Dell. Friend of Mr. Pickwick. 'A stout old gentleman in a blue coat and bright buttons.'—*The Pickwick Papers.*

WARDLE, MRS. Mother of Mr. Wardle. 'A very old lady in a lofty cap and faded silk gown.'—*The Pickwick Papers.*

WARDLE, EMILY. Daughter of Mr. Wardle, later the wife of Mr. Snodgrass. 'How dear Emily is flirting with the stranger gentleman!'—*The Pickwick Papers.*

WARDLE, ISABELLA. Daughter of Mr. Wardle, later the wife of Mr. Trundle. 'A very amiable and lovely girl.' —*The Pickwick Papers.*

WARDLE, MISS RACHEL. Sister of Mr. Wardle. 'A lady of uncertain age.'—*The Pickwick Papers.*

WEGG, SILAS. Ballad-monger and street seller, with a wooden leg. 'A knotty man, and a close-grained, with a face carved out of very hard material.'—*Our Mutual Friend.*

WELLER, SAM. Boots at the White Hart Inn, afterwards valet to Mr. Pickwick, and husband to Mary, the housemaid. 'I wonder whether I'm meant to be a foot-man; or a groom; or a game-keeper; or a seedsman; I looks like a compo' of every one of them.' —*The Pickwick Papers.*

Samuel Weller and Mary

WELLER, TONY. Coachman; father of Sam Weller. 'His face . . . had expanded, under the influence of good living, and a disposition remarkable for resignation.'—*The Pickwick Papers.*

WEMMICK, JOHN, JUNIOR. Confidential clerk to Mr. Jaggers. 'A dry man, rather short in stature . . . his mouth was such a post office of a mouth that he had a mechanical appearance of smiling.'—*Great Expectations.*

Tony Weller

WEMMICK, JOHN, SENIOR. *See* 'AGED, THE'—*Great Expectations.*

WESTLOCK, JOHN. Pupil of Mr. Pecksniff, later husband of Ruth Pinch. 'A good-looking youth, newly arrived at man's estate.'—*Martin Chuzzlewit.*

WHISKER. Mr. Garland's pony. 'Preserved his character for independence and principle down to the last moment of his life, which was an unusually long one.'—*The Old Curiosity Shop.*

WICKAM, MRS. Paul Dombey's nurse. 'Had a surprising natural gift of viewing all subjects in one utterly forlorn and pitiable light, and bringing dreadful precedents to bear upon them.'—*Dombey and Son.*

WICKFIELD, MR. Lawyer of Canterbury. 'There was a certain richness in his complexion, which I had been long accustomed . . . to connect with port wine.'—*David Copperfield.*

WICKFIELD, AGNES. His daughter. Later second wife of David Copperfield. 'Although her face was quite bright and happy, there was a tranquillity about it, and about her . . .'—*David Copperfield*.

WILDING, WALTER. A wine merchant, bearing the name of Wilding mistakenly. 'An innocent, open-speaking, unused-looking man.'—*No Thoroughfare*.

WILFER, BELLA. Daughter of Reginald Wilfer, later wife of John Hannon. 'With an exceedingly pretty figure and face, but with an impatient and petulant expression both in her face and in her shoulders.'—*Our Mutual Friend*.

WILFER, REGINALD. ('THE CHERUB'), office nickname 'Rumty'. Clerk in the firm of Chicksey, Veneering and Stobbles; father of Bella. 'His chubby, smooth, innocent appearance was a reason for his being always treated with condescension.'—*Our Mutual Friend*.

WILFER, MRS. 'Her lord being cherubic, she was necessarily majestic.'—*Our Mutual Friend*.

WILFER, LAVINIA. Younger sister of Bella. 'I'm not a child, to be taken notice of by strangers.'—*Our Mutual Friend*.

WILLET, JOE. Son of John Willet, later a soldier, husband of Dolly Varden, and landlord of the 'Maypole'. 'A broad-shouldered, strapping young fellow of twenty, whom it pleased his father still to consider a little boy.'—*Barnaby Rudge*.

WILLET, JOHN. Father of Joe; and landlord of the Maypole Inn. 'A fat face, which betokened profound obstinacy and slowness of apprehension; combined with a very strong reliance upon his own merits.'—*Barnaby Rudge*.

WINKLE, NATHANIEL. Member of the Pickwick Club. 'The sporting Winkle, communicating additional lustre to a new green shooting coat, plaid neckerchief, and closely fitting drabs.'—*The Pickwick Papers.*

WINKLE, MR. SENIOR. Father of Nathaniel. 'A little old gentleman . . . with a head and face the precise counterpart of those belonging to Mr. Winkle, Junior, excepting that he was rather bald.'—*The Pickwick Papers.*

WITHERDEN, MR. Solicitor to whom Abel Garland was articled. 'Short, chubby, fresh-coloured, brisk, and pompous.'—*The Old Curiosity Shop.*

WITHERFIELD, MISS. Whose room Mr. Pickwick mistook for his own at Ipswich. 'A middle-aged lady, in yellow curl-papers.'—*The Pickwick Papers.*

WITHERS. Page to Mrs. Skewton. 'When he stood upright he was tall, and wan, and thin.'—*Dombey and Son.*

WITITTERLY, MRS. JULIA. Kate Nickleby's employer. 'An air of sweet insipidity, and a face of engaging paleness.'—*Nicholas Nickleby.*

WOODCOURT, DR. ALLAN. Surgeon, later husband of Esther Summerson. 'The kindest physician in the college.' —*Bleak House.*

WOODCOURT, MRS. Mother of Dr. Allan. 'A pretty old lady with bright black eyes.'—*Bleak House.*

WOPSLE (stage name Waldengarver). A guest at Joe Gargery's. 'United to a Roman nose, and a large shining bald forehead, had a deep voice which he was uncommonly proud of.'—*Great Expectations.*

WRAYBURN, EUGENE. A briefless barrister, later husband of Lizzie Hexam. 'In susceptibility to boredom . . . I assure you I am the most consistent of mankind.' —*Our Mutual Friend*.

'WREN, JENNY.' *See* CLEAVER, FANNY—*Our Mutual Friend*.

ZEPHYR. A drunken prisoner, with Mr. Pickwick in the Fleet. 'Performing the most popular steps of a hornpipe, with a slang and burlesque caricature of grace and lightness.'—*The Pickwick Papers*.

PLOTS OF THE NOVELS
AND MAIN STORIES

INDEX TO PLOTS

As brisk as bees, if not altogether as light as fairies, did the four Pickwickians assemble on the morning of the twenty-second day of December, in the year of grace in which these, their faithfully-recorded adventures, were undertaken, and accomplished.

Samuel Pickwick, Esquire, is General Chairman and Member of The Pickwick Club, whose aims are research and jovial entertainment. Its headquarters are in London, but Mr. Pickwick obtains the consent of the members to take a small committee of friends with him on investigations far afield.

Tracy Tupman, Augustus Snodgrass and Nathaniel Winkle accompany him to Kent. Before starting on the journey, Mr. Pickwick is rescued from a bullying cabman by Alfred Jingle, a strolling player, who goes on with them to Rochester, where Mr. Winkle narrowly escapes fighting a duel. At a military review the four meet a Mr. Wardle, of Manor Farm, Dingley Dell, his two daughters, Isabella and Emily, his sister, Rachel Wardle, and Joe, the Fat Boy, their servant.

Wardle invites them to Manor Farm, where they go shooting. Winkle misses his bird and wings Tupman in the arm. Miss Wardle nurses him, and the susceptible Tupman proposes to her; but Jingle, interested in the lady's fortune, persuades her to elope with him. Wardle and Pickwick overtake them at the White Hart Inn, London, and Jingle is bribed to abandon his matrimonial ambitions.

At the inn, Pickwick encounters Sam Weller, the 'Boots', and takes him into his service as valet. Attempting to break this news to his landlady, Mrs. Bardell, he gives the mistaken impression that he is trying to propose marriage to her.

The Pickwickians' next journey is to Eatanswill. An

Mrs. Bardell faints in Mr. Pickwick's arms

election is in progress. They attend a party given by Mrs.
Leo Hunter, and once again meet Jingle. Pickwick chases
him this time to Bury St. Edmunds, but Jingle and his
servant-accomplice Job Trotter land Pickwick in an
embarrassing situation in a young ladies' boarding establishment.

After another visit to Dingley Dell, Pickwick and
friends return to London and Pickwick finds that Mrs.
Bardell has begun an action against him for breach of
promise. He journeys to Ipswich, mistakes the bedroom
of a lady traveller for his own, and is threatened by her
prospective fiancé. Pickwick is arrested, but released by
the wit of Sam Weller, and told by him that Jingle is now
masquerading under an aristocratic alias in Ipswich.
Pickwick unmasks Jingle to the magistrate.

At Christmas, the Pickwickians visit Dingley Dell for
the wedding of Mr. Wardle's daughter, Isabella, to

Christmas Eve at Mr. Wardle's

Trundle. Snodgrass has fallen in love with Emily Wardle, and Winkle with her friend, Arabella Allen. Two medical students, Bob Sawyer and Arabella's brother, Ben Allen, arrive. Bob is also in love with Arabella.

Back in London, Pickwick defends the breach of promise action, but loses, and Mrs. Bardell is awarded £750 damages. Pickwick refuses to pay, and goes to Bath, where he sees something of fashionable society, while

Sam mingles with the Bath footmen. Winkle has an unfortunate adventure involving a Mrs. Dowler and a sedan-chair, and leaves for Bristol, where he has news of Arabella. Pickwick and Sam follow him, and arrange a meeting between the lovers. Meanwhile, Sam has found himself a sweetheart in Mary, a pretty housemaid.

Pickwick steadfastly refuses to pay the damages, and is imprisoned in the Fleet, together with Sam, who has arranged for himself to be arrested as a debtor. In the prison they encounter Jingle and Trotter, also prisoners, and very much down on their luck. The generous Pickwick befriends them.

After three months in the Fleet, Pickwick meets Mrs. Bardell, who has been sent to prison for non-payment of her legal costs. Pickwick pays them for her, and she in turn agrees to forgo the damages. Pickwick, Sam, Jingle and Trotter leave the Fleet, Jingle to embark on a new life as an emigrant.

Pickwick is again involved in the affairs of Winkle, now married to Arabella, and reconciles both Ben Allen and Winkle's father to the marriage. Then Snodgrass develops amorous troubles: he has decided to elope with Emily Wardle. Her father agrees to the marriage, and the elopement is called off, in favour of a more conventional wedding.

The Pickwick Club is dissolved, and Pickwick retires to his home at Dulwich, attended by Sam, and later, after Sam's marriage, by his wife Mary and their children.

'Mr. Pickwick is somewhat infirm now; but he retains all his former juvenility of spirit . . . The children idolize him, and so indeed does the whole neighbourhood. Every year, he repairs to a large family merry-making at Mr. Wardle's; on this, as on all occasions, he is invariably attended by the faithful Sam, between whom and his master there exists a steady and reciprocal attachment which nothing but death will terminate.'

OLIVER TWIST

> *He was badged and ticketed, and fell into his place*
> *at once—a parish child—the orphan of a workhouse*
> *—the humble, half-starved drudge—to be cuffed and*
> *buffeted through the world—despised by all, and*
> *pitied by none.*

A vagrant young woman dies giving birth to a boy in a workhouse. The child is named Oliver Twist, and spends his life up to the age of nine in the workhouse orphanage. His 'sturdy spirit' emboldens him to protest against the meagre supply of gruel the boys are given, and his request for more gets him into severe trouble.

To get rid of him the Workhouse Board apprentice him to Sowerberry, an undertaker, but he again gets into trouble when he fights Noah Claypole, a bullying lad, for insulting his dead mother. Oliver runs away to London. In Barnet he encounters Jack Dawkins, known as 'The Artful Dodger', one of a gang of pickpockets organized by Fagin, a cunning Jew. The Dodger takes Oliver to Fagin, who sees possibilities in the bright little boy, and sends him out on a pocket-picking expedition with The Dodger and Charley Bates. Oliver is horrified when they pick the pocket of an old gentleman, Mr. Brownlow, and runs away. He is arrested, but Mr. Brownlow recognizes his innocence, takes him home and befriends him.

Fagin employs a burglar, Bill Sikes, and Nancy, his mistress, to recapture Oliver. Sikes takes Oliver as assistant to rob a house at Chertsey. The alarm is raised, and Oliver left wounded on the spot. He is taken into the house and befriended by its owner, Mrs. Maylie, and her adopted niece, Rose. They nurse him through his illness, and he becomes almost one of the family. He learns that Harry, Mrs. Maylie's son, is in love with Rose, but that she will not marry him because of some dark secret in her family history.

George Cruikshank.

Oliver asking for more

Fagin, meanwhile, is looking for Oliver, helped by 'Monks', a mysterious figure who seems to have a peculiar hatred of the child. Nancy, who has always been friendly towards Oliver, takes the risk of telling Rose Maylie of plots against Oliver. Her treachery is discovered by Noah Claypole, now one of Fagin's gang, and he reports to

Oliver's reception by Fagin and the boys

Fagin and Sikes. Sikes, furious, kills Nancy with a club. He flies from justice, followed by his dog, Bull's-eye, which will not leave him in spite of his brutality to it. After much miserable wandering he returns to London to hide, is traced through the dog and, in attempting to escape across a roof, is accidentally hanged.

Mr. Brownlow brings down justice on Fagin and his gang. Fagin is tried and executed. The Artful Dodger is transported, and Charley Bates reforms and becomes a farmer. Mr. Brownlow finds that Monks is really Oliver's half-brother, and that Oliver is the natural son of one Edwin Leeford and Agnes Fleming. Edwin Leeford is dead, but in his will left money to Oliver as well as to his legitimate son, Monks; hence Monks' desire to destroy

Oliver. Mr. Brownlow also learns from him that Rose Maylie is the sister of Oliver's mother, Agnes. The Parish Beadle, Bumble, and his wife are found guilty of complicity in the plot against Oliver, and lose their status in the workhouse, becoming inmates of it instead. Monks dies in prison.

Oliver is adopted by Mr. Brownlow; Harry Maylie and Rose marry, and all ends happily.

THE LIFE AND ADVENTURES OF NICHOLAS NICKLEBY

*Young men are adventurous. It is extraordinary
what they will rush upon, sometimes.*

Ralph Nickleby, miser and moneylender, of Golden Square, London, receives an application for financial help from his dead brother's wife, Mrs. Nickleby, and her son Nicholas and daughter Kate. He gives them a little, grudgingly. He dislikes young Nicholas on sight, and finds him a post as far away as possible—at one of the notorious 'Yorkshire schools', headmaster Mr. Wackford Squeers.

Dotheboys Hall is a dreadful place. The boys are ill-treated and neglected by their brutal and ignorant headmaster and his unpleasant family. Nicholas intervenes to save Smike, a poor drudge who has run away and been recaptured, from a thrashing. Squeers turns on him, Nicholas beats Squeers, and the school breaks up in disorder. Nicholas leaves in disgust, decides to walk to London, and is befriended by John Browdie, fiancé of Fanny Squeers' friend, Matilda Price. Smike follows Nicholas, begging to serve him. In London they are helped by Ralph Nickleby's eccentric clerk, Newman Noggs, who seeks revenge against Ralph.

Nicholas becomes tutor to the large family of Kenwigs daughters, while his sister Kate joins Madame Mantalini's

The internal economy of Dotheboys Hall

millinery establishment. Ralph sends two worthless noblemen, Sir Mulberry Hawk and Lord Frederick Verisopht, to pester Kate with attentions.

After a quarrel with Ralph, Nicholas leaves London, accompanied by Smike. They arrive at Portsmouth, and join the theatrical company of Mr. Vincent Crummles. Nicholas becomes an author and juvenile lead, and Smike plays character parts. They are recalled to London by a letter from Newman Noggs. Ralph has taken Kate away from Madame Mantalini's and found a situation for her with Mrs. Wititterly, a social climber. Nicholas hears Sir Mulberry Hawk referring insultingly to Kate, and thrashes him.

Kate and Mrs. Nickleby leave Ralph's house, and Nicholas breaks off all connection with his uncle. He removes Kate from the Wititterlys', and they all go to live temporarily with Miss La Creevy, a miniature portrait painter. Nicholas, looking for work, meets the kindly old Cheeryble Brothers, who engage him as assistant to Tim Linkinwater, their right-hand man. They also allow the Nickleby family to have a pleasant little cottage at a low rent.

Smike is recaptured in the street by Squeers, but rescued by John Browdie. Ralph and Squeers conspire against Smike, pretending to have found his father in Snawley, a hypocrite. They attempt to kidnap Smike, but John Browdie and Nicholas defeat them.

Romantic interests have developed for Kate, who is falling in love with Frank Cheeryble, nephew of the brothers; for Mrs. Nickleby, who is briefly courted by 'the Gentleman in Small-clothes' next-door; and for Nicholas, who loves Madeline Bray, the only support of her weak and sickly father. She is in Ralph's power—an elderly and repulsive acquaintance of his, the money-lender, Arthur Gride, possesses a deed relating to a legacy coming to her, and through it persuades her father to make her marry Gride. Only the arrival of Nicholas, and the sudden death of her father, save her from the marriage. Nicholas takes Madeline to his mother. Through the Cheerybles, she is proved to be a considerable heiress.

Smike, always weakly, dies, confessing at the last his hopeless love for Kate. It is discovered that he was the son of Ralph, by a secret marriage. Ralph had believed that the boy had died in childhood, and the discovery of the truth drives him to such remorse that he hangs himself. Gride and Snawley are arrested and Squeers imprisoned.

The 'Gentleman in Small-clothes' declares his passion for Mrs. Nickleby

Nicholas refuses to inherit Ralph's money, and will not propose to Madeline because she is now an heiress. Kate refuses Frank Cheeryble on similar grounds. But the Cheeryble Brothers sort out all these scruples: Nicholas, Frank and Tim Linkinwater become members of the firm, and three marriages take place—Nicholas to Madeline, Frank to Kate, and Tim to Miss La Creevy.

Squeers is sentenced to transportation, and Dotheboys Hall breaks up with frantic demonstrations. The boys attack Mrs. Squeers and scatter; it is the end of the school. Lord Frederick Verisopht is killed in a duel with Sir Mulberry Hawk, who flies to the Continent; Crummles and his family go to America. The affairs of the firm of Cheeryble and Nickleby flourish.

THE OLD CURIOSITY SHOP

> *I had ever before me the old dark murky rooms . . .*
> *the dust and rust and worm that lives in wood—*
> *and alone in the midst of all this lumber and decay*
> *and ugly age, the beautiful child in her gentle*
> *slumber, smiling through her light and sunny*
> *dreams.*

Mr. Trent lives at the Old Curiosity Shop in London, with his grand-daughter, Little Nell, who keeps house for him. The old man is a chronic gambler. He borrows money from Daniel Quilp, a dwarf, who sells him up. Terrified of Quilp, the old man and Nell run away. They encounter Codlin and Short, two Punch and Judy showmen, and travel with them for a time.

Then they meet a schoolmaster, who has just lost his favourite pupil. Nell takes the dead boy's place in his affections; but she and her grandfather move on, to join Jarley's Wax-works Show. The kindly Mrs. Jarley befriends them, and they are almost settled when the old

Nell asleep in the Old Curiosity Shop

man is lured into gambling by some card-sharpers. He
loses all their money. Nell makes him leave the place
where he has been tempted, and once again they set out on
their travels. After many trials and hardships they meet
once more their schoolmaster friend, who finds a home for
them. It is a strange old house near an ancient church.
The old man and the child are at peace, but Nell's health is
slowly fading after all her sufferings.

Meanwhile, two separate searches are being made for
the pair—by Quilp, who has offered rewards for finding
them, and by old Mr. Trent's brother. Calling himself
'The Single Gentleman', the brother goes to lodge with
Sampson Brass, a lawyer in league with Quilp. Here he
meets Kit Nubbles, a youth who admired Nell in her
Curiosity Shop days, and who now works at the house of
Mr. Garland in Finchley. The Single Gentleman and Kit
obtain a clue to Nell's whereabouts.

Quilp hates Kit, and tries to ruin him by getting Sampson Brass to prefer a false charge of theft against him. But the plot does not succeed: Brass is found out and sentenced, Quilp tries to escape, but is drowned, and Kit is set free. Sampson Brass's clerk, Dick Swiveller, an amiable tippler, who has been innocently implicated in the plot against Kit, becomes dangerously ill and is nursed back to health by the Brass's little maid-of-all-work, whom he has befriended and christened 'The Marchioness'.

The search for Nell is finally successful, but she is found too late; she has died only a short time before the joyful party arrives. Her grandfather is out of his mind with grief, and soon is found lying dead on Nell's grave.

Kit Nubbles marries Barbara, the Garlands' neat little maid. Dick Swiveller, a reformed character, sends his 'Marchioness' to a finishing school, under the name of Sophronia Sphinx; and, when she has grown to womanhood, marries her.

BARNABY RUDGE

I am often out before the sun, and travel home when he has gone to rest. I am away in the woods before the day has reached the shady places, and am often there when the bright moon is peeping through the boughs, and looking down upon the other moon that lives in the water.

The story begins in the year 1775, at the Maypole Inn, Chigwell, Essex. One of the friends of John Willet, the inn's dull, slow landlord, tells a visitor the story of the death of Mr. Reuben Haredale, twenty-two years earlier. This owner of the great house known as The Warren had been found murdered and robbed. His steward and gardener had both disappeared, and neither had been found—until months later, when the body of Rudge, the steward, was discovered.

Geoffrey Haredale, a Roman Catholic gentleman, brother of the murdered man, has also been suspected of the murder. He lives a retired, embittered life with his niece, Emma Haredale, and shows liking only for her company and that of Mary Rudge, widow of the steward.

Mrs. Rudge has a son, Barnaby, born the day after the murder. He is mentally retarded and much afraid of blood, but gentle and kindhearted. He has a pet talking raven, called Grip. Mrs. Rudge appears to fear a mysterious stranger who visits her, and who commits a highway robbery the same night that he hears the story of the murder. Mrs. Rudge and Barnaby leave the district, and disappear for five years.

Emma Haredale is in love with Edward Chester, son of Sir John Chester, an enemy of Haredale. Sir John and Haredale sink their differences sufficiently to combine in causing a rift between the two young people. Edward quarrels with Emma and leaves England.

Another romance is thwarted, this time between Joe Willet, son of the landlord of the Maypole, and Dolly Varden, the pretty daughter of a London locksmith, Gabriel Varden. Dolly is also pursued by Hugh, an uncouth young ostler at the Maypole. She coquettishly refuses Joe, who enlists as a soldier and is sent to America. Dolly becomes companion to Emma Haredale. Dolly's mother, a peevish, contrary character, has opposed the match, aided by Miggs, her maid, a jealous and vinegary spinster in love with Varden's apprentice Sim Tappertit. But Sim prefers his master's daughter, and plots darkly how to win her.

The story moves on to 1780, when Lord George Gordon, the Protestant fanatic, begins his 'No Popery' movement and incites a mob to riots in London. The Rudges are now in London, and Barnaby joins the rioters. The mob surges out to Chigwell. The Warren, being a Catholic house, is destroyed, and Emma and Dolly are

Dolly Varden and Hugh of the Maypole Inn

kidnapped—Dolly by Sim Tappertit. Haredale returns to the Warren to look for Emma. He finds instead none other than Rudge, the steward thought to have been murdered many years before. It is discovered that Rudge had murdered Reuben Haredale and also the gardener, whose body he had disguised as his own. He has since been in hiding, and has consistently terrorized his wife in case she gave away his secret.

Rudge is imprisoned in Newgate, but the rioters break in and release the prisoners. The riots are quelled, and arrests are made—among them that of Barnaby. Emma and Dolly are set free by Geoffrey Haredale, Edward Chester, and Joe Willet—the latter returned from the

Savannahs, less one arm. He marries Dolly; Edward
marries Emma and goes to the West Indies with her. Joe
goes home to Chigwell to find the Maypole much battered
by the mob, and his father childish from shock.

Barnaby's father is hanged, and Barnaby receives the
same sentence, but is pardoned with the aid of Gabriel

Barnaby Rudge in prison

Varden. His mentality improves, and he and his mother, freed from the shadow of Rudge, retire happily to the farm of the Maypole.

Sir John Chester is killed in a duel with Geoffrey Haredale, who goes abroad and dies there. Hugh of the Maypole, one of the rioters to be hanged, proves to have been Sir John's natural son by a gipsy woman. Mrs. Varden improves as a result of the shock of Dolly's capture, and becomes consistently cheerful; while Sim Tappertit has his shapely legs crushed during the mob's violence. Miggs, disappointed in her ambition to marry Sim, becomes a female turnkey.

THE LIFE AND ADVENTURES OF MARTIN CHUZZLEWIT.

> *All hail to the vessel of Pecksniff the sire!*
> *And favouring breezes to fan;*
> *While Tritons flock round it, and proudly admire*
> *The architect, artist, and man!*

Martin Chuzzlewit the Elder is much sought after by his relatives because of his wealth. But he associates only with young Martin Chuzzlewit, his grandson, and the girl Mary Graham, who acts as companion to him. When Martin and Mary fall in love and wish to marry, the old man is displeased, as he wanted to arrange the match himself. Young Martin takes himself off to become an apprentice to Mr. Pecksniff, Architect and Surveyor of Salisbury, arch-hypocrite, and passer-off of his apprentices' work as his own. Pecksniff is delighted to capture the services of Martin whom he sees as a possible husband for one of his two daughters, Charity (the vinegary) and Mercy (the frivolous). Martin is attracted by neither, but becomes friendly with Tom Pinch, an honest little old–young person who works for Pecksniff and loyally will hear nothing but good of the man.

Mr. Pecksniff and his charming daughters with Tom Pinch

Old Martin persuades Pecksniff to get rid of his grand-son. Martin decides to go to America. Mark Tapley, a jolly ostler from the Blue Dragon Inn, reluctantly parts from Mrs. Lupin, the buxom landlady, to accompany Martin, feeling that the inn is too cheerful a place to give him scope for being jolly in trying circumstances.

Circumstances in America prove very trying indeed; for Martin and Mark, travelling to the supposedly rising town

Mark Tapley leaves the Blue Dragon

of Eden, where Martin hopes to become an architect, find it little more than a fever-ridden swamp.

In England, Pecksniff has lost no time in getting on the right side of old Martin. He takes Charity and Mercy to London, to stay at Mrs. Todgers' boarding-house. Jonas Chuzzlewit, their cousin, invites them to dine with old Anthony Chuzzlewit, his father, brother of old Martin. Jonas, a thorough villain with an eye to the main chance, buys poison to put in his father's medicine. Soon afterwards the old man dies. His old servant, Chuffey, is prostrated with grief for his master's loss, and in his ravings accuses Jonas of having killed him. Chuffey is nursed by Mrs. Sarah Gamp, professional nurse and midwife, and comic relief in the story, who also nurses Lewsome, a doctor's assistant who has sold the poison to Jonas. Pecksniff takes charge of the funeral arrangements, and Jonas proposes marriage to Mercy, who dislikes him but accepts in a spirit of silly coquetry. He marries her, and treats her so brutally that her frivolous manner and outlook drop away and she becomes a sad, frightened woman.

Jonas becomes a director and shareholder of the Anglo-Bengalee Disinterested Loan and Life Insurance Company, a swindling business organized by one Tigg Montague, alias Montague Tigg. Tigg makes enquiries which reveal that Jonas is suspected of having murdered his father. Tigg uses this knowledge to blackmail Jonas into getting Pecksniff to invest money in the company. To keep his secret, Jonas murders Tigg and hides the body in a lonely wood.

Pecksniff makes overtures to Mary Graham, who, with old Martin, is now staying at the Pecksniff residence. Mary goes to Tom Pinch for help, and Tom is at last disillusioned in Pecksniff, who dismisses him. Tom goes to London and there meets John Westlock, once a pupil of Pecksniff's. Tom removes his pretty sister Ruth from her uncongenial situation as governess. They find lodgings together, in Islington; and Tom, by the help of some unknown benefactor, becomes a librarian.

In America, Martin and Mark Tapley have been dangerously ill with swamp-fever. They recover and return to England. Martin goes to his grandfather to ask forgiveness for his past behaviour. But Pecksniff intervenes, and Martin returns to London, where he meets Tom Pinch and John Westlock and learns about Jonas's activities. Mrs. Gamp is employed to confront Jonas with Lewsome. Jonas is charged with the murder of his father, clears himself, but is further accused of having killed Tigg. On his way to prison he poisons himself.

Tom Pinch's secret benefactor proves to be old Martin, who calls a meeting in his library to which are summoned young Martin and Mary, Mark Tapley and Mrs. Lupin, Tom Pinch, Ruth Pinch and John Westlock, and Pecksniff. At this meeting all issues are resolved. Pecksniff is suitably punished for his hypocrisy, Martin and Mary receive the old man's blessing, and the other two couples are dispatched towards matrimony.

Pecksniff becomes a begging-letter writer. Mercy takes Mary's place as companion to old Martin. Charity almost achieves matrimony with Mr. Moddle, a boarder at Todgers', but he escapes her at the altar.

DEALINGS WITH THE FIRM OF DOMBEY AND SON

They do say . . . that his mind's so set all the while upon having his son in the House, that although he's only a baby now, he's going to have balances struck oftener than formerly, and the books kept closer than they used to be.

Paul Dombey, Senior, is the proud, unbending head of Dombey's, a large mercantile house in London. He is delighted when his wife presents him with a son, for they have previously only had a daughter, Florence, who is quite unimportant in her father's eyes. Mrs. Dombey dies, not particularly to Dombey's regret, for he now has Paul Junior to bring up as inheritor and partner in the firm. Paul is utterly unlike his father—a gentle, dreamy, delicate child, with a deep love for his sister, who in turn is tenderly protective towards him.

Paul is sent to Brighton at the age of six for the health-giving air. After a brief stay at Mrs. Pipchin's house he is sent to Dr. Blimber's school, and, in spite of kindly and considerate treatment, he very soon dies. His death drives Florence and her father even more apart, for in his angry grief he resents her very existence.

The neglected little girl is one day lost in the streets of London, and is found by Walter Gay, a boy employed by Dombey and Son, after she has been the captive of a sinister old woman calling herself 'Good Mrs. Brown'. Walter lives with his uncle, Solomon Gills, a ships' instrument-seller, who is friendly with Captain Cuttle, a one-armed seaman. Walter and Florence become friends; she has no other companions but Susan Nipper, her sharp young maid, and the clumsy dog, Diogenes, who had been a pet of little Paul in Brighton.

Walter, who has made an enemy of the manager of Dombey's, James Carker, who wants him out of the way, is sent abroad. Months pass without news of him, and his uncle goes in search of him, leaving Captain Cuttle in charge of the shop.

Dombey, meanwhile, has been introduced by Major Joseph Bagstock to Edith Granger, a proud and beautiful young widow, whom he has married. The union is a cold-hearted one on both sides, but Edith develops an affection for Florence, which is returned. Dombey resents their friendship. He goads Edith until in revenge she elopes with James Carker to France, but soon leaves him. Carker is accidentally killed by a train. His death is a form of poetic

Paul and Mrs. Pipchin

justice for having years ago cast off Alice Marwood,
Edith's physical double, daughter to that 'Good Mrs.
Brown' who had held Florence captive.

Florence, now grown up, tries to make friends with and
comfort her father, but he gives her angry words and **a**

blow. She flies from the house in despair and takes refuge at the shop of Sol Gills. Gills is still away, but Captain Cuttle receives her kindly and entertains her with a long story of two people who are sitting as they are when a shadow on the wall startles them. Florence looks round, and sees just such a shadow. It is that of Walter, returned safe and sound. Walter and Florence marry and go on a long voyage. A year later, Dombey's becomes bankrupt and Dombey himself is a broken man. As he broods remorsefully on the past, Florence appears, returned from abroad, and again offers him her love, telling him that now she has a son—another Paul. At last Dombey's reserve is broken, and he spends the rest of his life happily with Florence and her family.

DAVID COPPERFIELD

If it should appear from anything I may set down in this narrative that I was a child of close observation, or that as a man I have a strong memory of my childhood, I undoubtedly lay claim to both these characteristics.

At Blunderstone, in Suffolk, young David Copperfield is born, a posthumous child. His eccentric great-aunt, Miss Betsey Trotwood, arrives at the house that night, but leaves in a temper on hearing that the baby is a boy, not a girl.

David grows up in the care of Clara Peggotty, his nurse, and his pretty, girlish mother. Then Mrs. Copperfield marries again, one Mr. Murdstone. David is sent for a holiday to Yarmouth, where lives Daniel Peggotty, Clara Peggotty's brother, a kindly, honest fisherman. Living with him are Mrs. Gummidge, a 'lone, lorn' widow, Little Em'ly, Peggotty's pretty niece, and her boyish sweetheart, Ham, Peggotty's nephew.

David is hospitably received by Mr. Peggotty

David returns home to find things changed for the worse. Murdstone is a stern, heartless man with no affection for David, and, abetted by his sister Jane Murdstone, makes the little boy's life a misery. David is not sorry to go to boarding-school, but is not happy when he gets there, as the headmaster, Creakle, is a bully and a beater. But David finds two friends—James Steerforth, the handsome head boy, and the comic Tommy Traddles. He is shocked by the news that his mother has died and he returns home. Barkis, a taciturn carrier who drives his horse and cart round the country lanes, has matrimonial aspirations to Clara Peggotty and eventually marries her.

A further period of misery begins. David is sent by his step-father to work at a bottling firm, where he is deeply unhappy. There is a certain amount of light relief about his lodgings, for he stays with the optimistic Mr. Wilkins Micawber, always impecunious but always expecting something advantageous to turn up. David's misery at work finally drives him into running away. He walks from London to Dover, and finds his great-aunt, Betsey Trotwood, who takes him under her protection. He makes the acquaintance of the simple-minded Mr. Dick, who lives with her. The Murdstones demand David's return, but Miss Trotwood sends them about their business.

Miss Trotwood sends him to school at Canterbury, where his schoolmaster is Dr. Strong, and where he lives with Mr. Wickfield, a lawyer, who has one daughter, Agnes, a calm, gentle girl with whom David becomes friendly. Wickfield has a clerk, Uriah Heep, a fawning, mock-humble individual who is gradually gaining power over his master.

David leaves school, and goes to stay with the Peggottys accompanied by Steerforth. Little Em'ly is now engaged to Ham, but Steerforth persuades her to elope with him, and they go abroad, pursued by Daniel Peggotty.

David becomes a clerk in the law firm of Spenlow and

Barkis and Clara Peggotty drive off to their wedding

Jorkins, and falls desperately in love with Dora Spenlow, daughter of one of the partners. David is anxious to better his financial prospects as his great-aunt has fallen on bad times. He studies shorthand and becomes a Parliamentary reporter, marrying Dora when her father dies.

Dora proves a charming but domestically inadequate wife, and the home of the young couple is in a sad state of

The interview between Miss Trotwood and the Murdstones

muddle, in spite of which David begins to make a name for himself as an author.

Daniel Peggotty has found Em'ly, ruined but repentant, and the family decide to emigrate to Australia. Barkis has died and Clara is a widow. There are changes at Canterbury: Wickfield and Agnes have fallen more and more into the power of Uriah Heep, but Micawber, who has learnt of Heep's plotting, betrays him. Heep is forced to give up all he has gained, which includes the property of Miss Trotwood. Micawber decides to join the Peggotty family in their emigration, and a more prosperous future lies ahead for him there. Steerforth is drowned in a storm, and Ham Peggotty dies in an attempt to save him.

Dora dies, and David, now a successful author, travels for three years, returns, and marries Agnes, who has always loved him, thereby fulfilling Dora's last wish.

BLEAK HOUSE

> *Never can there come fog too thick, never can there come mud and mire too deep, to assort with the groping and floundering condition which this High Court of Chancery, most pestilent of hoary sinners, holds this day, in the sight of heaven and earth.*

Esther Summerson tells her own story. She has been brought up by Miss Barbary, her godmother, really her aunt, who will not acknowledge her relationship because Esther is illegitimate. After six years' teaching at Miss Donny's school, Esther goes to live with her guardian, John Jarndyce, the master of Bleak House. There is a Jarndyce suit in the Court of Chancery which has dragged out interminably. One of the principals, Tom Jarndyce, has committed suicide, and John Jarndyce refuses to be associated with the case. But he has taken into his home two of the parties of the suit—the young, pretty Ada Clare, and the irresponsible youth Richard Carstone. Ada and Richard are in love, but Jarndyce will not allow them to marry until they are of age, and Richard capable of earning his living. Richard, however, pins his hopes on the success of the lawsuit, and will not concentrate on any of the professions which in turn he takes up.

Jarndyce and the two young people develop a warm affection for Esther, who runs Bleak House with gentle efficiency, christened 'Dame Durden' by Jarndyce. She meets Dr. Allan Woodcourt, a young surgeon, and knows herself to be in love with him, but without hope of marrying him.

Through a friend of Jarndyce, Lawrence Boythorn, Esther meets Sir Leicester Dedlock, a courtly old gentleman, and his beautiful wife. Her manner is cold and haughty, but there is a secret in her life. Tulkinghorn, the family solicitor, determines to find it out. He hears of Lady Dedlock being shown a London burial-ground where one 'Nemo', otherwise Captain Hawdon, a legal copying-clerk, is buried. His suspicions are aroused. He seeks out Hawdon's old orderly and discovers that Hawdon was once Lady Dedlock's lover, and that Esther is their child. Lady Dedlock learns of the discovery of her secret from Guppy, a law clerk in love with Esther, and realizes for the first time that Esther is her daughter.

Esther contracts small-pox and loses all her beauty. She meets Lady Dedlock, who acknowledges her and asks her forgiveness. Richard Carstone leaves the army and secretly marries Ada. Esther receives a proposal of marriage from Jarndyce, and her affection for him causes her to accept, though she still loves Allan Woodcourt.

Tulkinghorn, who has been threatening Lady Dedlock, is found shot, and Lady Dedlock is suspected, as well as Hawdon's ex-orderly, Mr. George. He proves his innocence, but Lady Dedlock flies. Bucket, a detective, seeks her, with Esther's help, to tell her that her husband forgives her and wants her to return to him. They find her dead at the gate of the burial-ground where Hawdon lies.

Jarndyce finds out that Esther and Allan Woodcourt are in love, and gives her up to Allan with his blessing. The Jarndyce suit comes to an end at last, but the costs have swallowed up the whole of the money. Richard dies,

in poverty and disappointment. Ada returns to Bleak House
with her child.

HARD TIMES

> *You are to be in all things regulated and governed
> . . . by fact. We hope to have, before long, a board of
> fact, composed of commissioners of fact, who will
> force the people to be a people of fact, and of nothing
> but fact.*

Facts rule the Gradgrind family, and Fancy is strictly
kept out of their home. Thomas Gradgrind brings up his
children, Louisa and Tom, within the sphere of realities.
Cecilia Jupe, called Sissy, daughter of a circus performer,
joins the family. Josiah Bounderby, self-made man and
owner of the Coketown mills, admires Louisa, and ultimately marries her. Tom is given a position in Bounderby's
bank, and begins to sponge on his sister.

Louisa's marriage is not happy, and she finds an admirer
in James Harthouse, a man of the world who has come to
Coketown on political business. Tom robs the bank,
pretends that an outside break-in has occurred, and throws
the guilt of it on Stephen Blackpool, a recently discharged
mill-hand, notable for his forthrightness and honesty.
Louisa suspects that Tom is connected with the robbery,
and Blackpool's friend, Rachael, is determined to prove
him innocent. Blackpool and Rachael are in love, but he is
already married to a drunken, degraded wife.

Bounderby has a housekeeper, Mrs. Sparsit, who had
herself ambitions to marry him. She overhears James
Harthouse and Louisa planning to elope, and decides to
make capital out of this by telling Bounderby about it.
But Louisa, instead of eloping, goes to her father and talks
to him about her unhappy married life. When Bounderby
learns of the intended elopement, he goes to Thomas

Gradgrind's to tell him about it, but finds his wife with her father. Bounderby and Louisa agree to part, and Harthouse leaves Coketown. Louisa learns from Sissy Jupe to live outside the sphere of Fact.

Rachael writes to Stephen Blackpool, telling him to come back, but he does not reply. He is found after some days down a disused mine-shaft, dying, but manages to give Gradgrind a hint of the truth about his son. Gradgrind follows Tom, who escapes abroad, where he dies. Mrs. Sparsit finds that Bounderby's mother is a woman in humble circumstances, called Mrs. Pegler, and accordingly abandons her scheme for marrying him.

Gradgrind reforms, and makes his facts and figures subservient to Faith, Hope and Charity.

LITTLE DORRIT

> *With no earthly friend to help her ... with no knowledge even of the common daily tone and habits of the common members of the free community who are not shut up in prisons ... the Child of the Marshalsea began her womanly life.*

Arthur Clennam returns from India to his home, a rambling ancient house in the City of London. His supposed mother, Mrs. Clennam, a hard, stern old invalid, manages a commission business with the help of her old servant, Jeremy Flintwinch. Also employed by Mrs. Clennam is a little sempstress, Amy Dorrit, known affectionately as 'Little Dorrit'. She is the younger daughter of William Dorrit, called 'The Father of the Marshalsea' from the length of his imprisonment for debt in the Marshalsea Prison. Little Dorrit works as a sempstress to help her father and her brother Edward ('Tip') and sister Fanny.

Clennam is interested in her, and makes enquiries at the

Mrs. Clennam, Flintwinch and Arthur

'Circumlocution Office' about her family history. The Barnacle family—Lord Decimus Tite Barnacle, Mr. Tite Barnacle, and others—rules this office. In the course of his enquiries Clennam meets Daniel Doyce, an inventor, and they become partners. Clennam is romantically interested in Minnie Meagles ('Pet'), the pretty spoilt daughter of doting parents; but she marries Henry Gowan, an artist, and goes abroad with him.

Clennam renews contact with an old sweetheart of his, Flora Finching, now a widow, but is deeply disappointed to find how silly and affected she has become. He tries to help William Dorrit, who comes into wealth and is able to leave the Marshalsea and take his family travelling on the Continent.

William Dorrit, Fanny and Edward have all become spoilt by riches; only Little Dorrit has remained the same, and is still Clennam's friend, though the rest of her family ignore him. Fanny marries Sparkler, a friend of Henry Gowan. Her father engages a formidable lady called Mrs. General as chaperon for his daughters, and she has almost achieved her ambition of becoming their step-mother when William Dorrit dies.

After his death it is found that he has left his money in trust to a banker, Merdle, much given to speculation and even to swindling. Merdle commits suicide, and the Dorrits find they have lost all their wealth. Clennam has also been swindled, and is imprisoned for debt in the Marshalsea. Little Dorrit visits, comforts and nurses him in illness, and love develops between them. Doyce and Meagles come to his rescue; he is released, and marries Little Dorrit.

Mrs. Clennam confesses that Arthur is not her son, but the child of her dead husband's mistress, and that she has brought him up in a spirit of revenge. An adventurer called Rigaud, alias Blandois, who has been trying to blackmail her, is killed when the Clennam mansion crumbles into ruins. Mrs. Clennam dies shortly afterwards.

A TALE OF TWO CITIES

> *It was the spring of hope, it was the winter of despair, we had everything before us, we had nothing before us . . . in short, the period was so far like the present period . . .*

The story opens in the year 1775. Jarvis Lorry, agent of Tellson & Co., bankers, has gone to Paris to find Doctor

Alexandre Manette, a French physician who had been imprisoned in the Bastille for eighteen years. He is joined in his search by Lucie Manette, Dr. Manette's daughter, and they find the old man half-mad, making shoes. They bring him to London, where he regains his health and lost memory, though he remains prone to occasional relapses.

Five years later a trial takes place in London—that of Charles Darnay, nephew of the Marquis de St. Evremonde, on a charge of spying. He is acquitted, partly because of his resemblance to Sydney Carton, a lawyer present in the court.

Both Darnay and Carton are in love with Lucie. Carton, an irresponsible and dissolute character, tells Lucie he loves her, and offers to make any sacrifice for her that will make her happy. She marries Darnay.

In France, the Revolution is breaking out. Darnay's uncle is murdered and his home fired by the mob, who threaten to kill Gabelle, his tax and rent collector. Gabelle writes to Charles Darnay asking for protection, and Darnay, unknown to Lucie, goes to France.

1792—and Darnay is in the hands of the revolutionaries. He is imprisoned on suspicion of being an aristocrat. Lucie and Dr. Manette go to his help, and Dr. Manette is welcomed because of his past imprisonment in the Bastille. Because of this, Darnay is released, but is rearrested the same day on a new charge, through the influence of Madame Defarge, a grim revolutionary leader, wife of a wine-seller.

Darnay is sentenced to be guillotined. Sydney Carton arrives, and makes his way into the prison because he has recognized one of the turnkeys as a spy. He drugs Darnay and changes clothes with him. Because of his likeness to Darnay, the substitution is not noticed by the prison officers, and Carton goes to the guillotine in place of Darnay. Thus he carries out his promise to make any

The sea rises

sacrifice for Lucie's happiness. Lucie, with Darnay, Dr. Manette and Lorry, escapes to England.

There are sub-plots concerning Jerry Cruncher, bank-messenger and body-snatcher, and his family; and the enmity between Lucie's maid, Miss Pross, and the formidable Madame Defarge, whom Miss Pross finally kills, rendering herself deaf for life by the shot with which Madame Defarge's life is ended.

Great Expectations

> *'Biddy,' said I, after binding her to secrecy, 'I want to be a gentleman.'*
> *'Oh, I wouldn't, if I was you!' she returned. 'I don't think it would answer.'*

Philip Pirrip, called Pip, tells his own story. He has been born in a Kent village in the marsh country, beside the river, and brought up by his sister, wife of Joe Gargery the blacksmith. Pip's childhood is not happy, as Mrs. Joe is an inflexible and tyrannical woman. One evening Pip has a terrifying adventure in the marshes when he meets an escaped convict, who frightens him into smuggling out food from his sister's pantry. Next day the convict is recaptured.

Pip is taken by Joe Gargery's Uncle Pumblechook to visit Miss Havisham. She is an eccentric who dresses permanently as a bride and sits among the relics of an unconsumed wedding feast, for as a girl she had been deserted at the altar. Miss Havisham has a beautiful protégée, Estella, whom she is bringing up to despise men and humiliate them in revenge for her own wrongs. Pip, even at this early age, is attracted by Estella.

He now becomes apprentice to Joe at the forge, and there makes an enemy of Orlick, Joe's journeyman. Mrs.

Gargery is assaulted and left for dead by an unknown attacker; she is nursed in her illness by Biddy, a childhood friend of Pip's.

After four years at the forge Pip receives news from Jaggers, a London lawyer, that he has come into money from an unknown benefactor. He goes to London, and begins to lead an easy life. Matthew Pocket, related to Miss Havisham, is his tutor, and Pocket's son Herbert becomes Pip's best friend. At this time Pip is under the delusion that Miss Havisham wishes him to marry Estella. He lives on his capital, with no inclination to work for his living. His sister dies.

After he has come of age, Pip discovers that his unknown benefactor is the convict whom he had encountered as a boy. This man, Abel Magwitch, has escaped, and Pip hides him in a house near the Thames, taking Herbert Pocket into the secret.

Compeyson, another ex-convict, Magwitch's enemy and the betrayer of Miss Havisham, learns of Magwitch's hiding-place. Orlick (who was Mrs. Gargery's attacker) tries to murder Pip. Pip and Herbert take Magwitch down the river by boat, to smuggle him out of the country; but Compeyson and the police appear. In the ensuing fight, Compeyson is drowned and Magwitch seriously injured. He is sentenced to death, but dies in prison.

Pip becomes ill, and is nursed by Joe Gargery, who pays his debts for him. On recovering, Pip realizes that the possession of wealth had corrupted him, and decides to lead a more useful life. He joins Herbert Pocket in business in Cairo. In England, Estella, who is really the daughter of Magwitch, marries Pip's schoolfellow Bentley Drummle, and leads an unhappy life until he dies. Joe marries the kindly Biddy.

Pip returns after eleven years, and meets Estella, finding her much softened and wishing to be friends. He foresees that in time she will marry him.

OUR MUTUAL FRIEND

> *It is a sensation not experienced by many mortals*
> *. . . to be looking into a churchyard on a wild windy*
> *night, and to feel that I no more hold a place among*
> *the living than these dead do.*

Harmon, a dust contractor, has amassed a fortune and died while his estranged son, John Harmon, was abroad. He leaves him the greater part of his fortune on condition that he marries Bella Wilfer, daughter of a clerk. The rest of the money is left to Mr. and Mrs. Boffin, family servants. John Harmon arrives in England only to be attacked and knocked out by robbers. He escapes drowning, but a man of similar build, whose body is found in the river, is identified as John. John, seeing his chance to investigate the destiny forced upon him by his father, decides to take the name of Julius Handford, but later changes this to John Rokesmith.

Under this name he goes to lodge at the house of Reginald Wilfer, Bella's father, a cherubic individual deeply devoted to his daughter. Rokesmith visits Mr. and Mrs. Boffin, whom he had known as a child and who then had a great affection for him; but they do not recognize him. On his supposed death, they have inherited all his estate, and are leading a life of opulence as a result. Boffin makes John his secretary, and also takes Bella Wilfer into his household. John proposes marriage to her, but she tells him that she intends to marry money. The Boffins are frustrated in their attempts to find a boy orphan to adopt, to take the place of the young John Harmon whom they loved so many years ago.

The body wrongly identified as John's had been found by 'Gaffer' Hexam, a boatman, who has a daughter Lizzie and a son Charley. A young lawyer, Eugene Wrayburn, visits the Hexams and begins to fall in love with Lizzie. Hexam is accused of the murder of John Harmon by

'Rogue' Riderhood, a former partner, but is accidentally drowned. Lizzie goes to live with a little crippled girl, Fanny Cleaver, who calls herself Jenny Wren and is a dolls' dressmaker, the only support of her drunken father. Charley Hexam turns against Wrayburn, and is abetted in this by Bradley Headstone, his schoolmaster. Headstone falls in love with Lizzie. Lizzie goes for protection to Riah, a benevolent Jew, friend of Jenny Wren, who finds Lizzie a job at a mill. Wrayburn seeks her in vain.

The scene moves to the world of London fashion. The Veneerings are *nouveaux riches*, friends of Mr. and Mrs. Alfred Lammle, who have been tricked into marrying each other for money. They tell Boffin that Rokesmith is an adventurer. But Boffin and his wife know Rokesmith's secret, for Mrs. Boffin has at last recognized the boy in the man. In order to soften Bella and change her worldly point of view, Boffin pretends to persecute John, and finally turns him out of the house. Bella, in sympathy, goes too. She at last declares her love for John, and they are secretly married, with the blessing of Bella's father, setting up house in a small cottage in Blackheath.

Wrayburn, meanwhile, has found Lizzie Hexam. He contrives a meeting with her, but is afterwards attacked and severely injured by Headstone. Lizzie rescues him from the river, nurses him, and marries him when he appears to be dying. He recovers. Headstone is blackmailed by Riderhood, and in a fight by a river lock both are drowned.

A will is found by Silas Wegg, a ballad-monger, which appears to leave old Harmon's fortune to the Crown; but Boffin discovers a later one naming himself and his wife. He makes over all the money to John and Bella, and they move from Blackheath to his own London house, with their newly-born daughter.

Sub-plots are concerned with Betty Higden, an old working-woman terrified of the workhouse; Mortimer

Lightwood, a solicitor; the Podsnaps, friends of the Veneerings, and Mr. Venus, the taxidermist, admirer of Riderhood's daughter, Pleasant.

THE MYSTERY OF EDWIN DROOD (unfinished novel)

> *The woman's words are in the rising wind, in the angry sky, in the troubled water, in the flickering lights. There is some solemn echo of them even in the Cathedral chime . . . And so he goes up the postern stair.*

The story begins in a London opium-den, kept by an old woman known as 'Princess Puffer'. John Jasper, choir-master of Cloisterham, a cathedral town of Kent, is recovering from an opium-dream of Eastern splendours.

The scene moves to Cloisterham. Jasper is expecting a visit from his nephew, Edwin Drood, a young student of engineering, who is about to go to Egypt. Edwin is engaged to Rosa Bud, a charming orphan who is a boarder at Miss Twinkleton's Seminary for Young Ladies, the Nuns' House. Edwin and Rosa have been betrothed from childhood, under the terms of their fathers' wills, but they have an affection for each other which is more like that of brother and sister than of lovers. Jasper, though he professes great love for his nephew, is clearly in love with Rosa himself and is violently jealous of the young man, a fact of which Edwin seems to have no idea.

Two visitors arrive: Neville and Helena Landless, twins from Ceylon, a handsome, if mysterious pair. Their guardian, Mr. Honeythunder, has sent for them to complete their education in England. Neville is to study under Mr. Crisparkle, the cathedral's minor canon, and Helena at the Nuns' House. Rosa and Helena become friends, but there is antagonism between Edwin and Neville, which is encouraged by Jasper.

End of term at Miss Twinkleton's

On Christmas Eve the situation comes to a head. Unknown to Jasper, Rosa and Edwin make up their minds to break their engagement. Neville and Edwin attend a party at Jasper's, after quarrelling. Next morning Edwin has disappeared. Neville is suspected, as having been the last person to see Edwin, but he says that after they parted Edwin returned to Jasper's. Only Crisparkle believes in the innocence of his pupil. Jewellery belonging to Edwin is found in the river, and Neville comes under even darker suspicion.

Edwin, unknown to anyone, had collected a ring

belonging to Rosa before his disappearance, but this is not with the other jewellery.

Jasper proposes to Rosa. Frightened, she goes to her guardian, Mr. Grewgious, a lawyer of Staple Inn. Helena and Neville also go to London, where they meet Lieutenant Tartar, a personable young naval man whose admiration for Rosa is obvious.

In Cloisterham, a visitor has arrived—Mr. Datchery, a genial gentleman of leisure, and of somewhat strange appearance, suggesting a disguise. He appears deeply interested in the vanishing of Edwin Drood, and follows up clues to the mystery. He keeps a score of his successes in this field, adding a particularly thick line to it when he discovers a connection between Jasper and Princess Puffer.

Here the story abruptly ends, for Dickens died when the book was only about a quarter finished. There has been a strong hint that Durdles, a stonemason, will in time detect an extra body in one of the cathedral tombs.

CHRISTMAS BOOKS

1. A CHRISTMAS CAROL IN PROSE, being a Ghost Story of Christmas

Ebenezer Scrooge is the surviving partner in the firm of Scrooge and Marley; Marley has been dead seven years. Scrooge is a grasping old miser, with no kind or generous impulses in his nature, even at Christmas. His poor clerk, Bob Cratchit, is paid the lowest possible wage on which to keep himself and his large family. Scrooge replies to all Christmas greetings with scorn, regarding the whole thing as 'humbug'.

Going to bed on Christmas Eve, he is taking his gruel when he is visited by the ghost of Marley, in grave-clothes and dragging a chain. He tells Scrooge that this chain is self-forged of his misdeeds in life, for he had only applied

Marley's ghost

himself to the getting of money, not realizing that mankind itself was his business. He warns Scrooge that the same fate lies ahead of him, and that he is being given three chances to escape it. He will be haunted by Three Spirits.

The First Spirit arrives, a curious ageless figure. It is the Ghost of Christmas Past, and it conducts Scrooge through scenes of his childhood and youth, bringing him remorse for opportunities wasted and the substitution of ambition for love in his life.

Next night, the Second Spirit arrives: the Ghost of Christmas Present, a jolly giant. It takes Scrooge to the poor home of the Cratchit family, poverty-stricken but happy, even though the youngest child, Tiny Tim, is a hopeless cripple who may not live long. It shows him how people everywhere are rejoicing in Christmas, and how his own family laugh good-naturedly at his attitude to it. As it leaves him the Spirit reveals, clinging to its skirts, the spectres of Ignorance and Want, in the form of wretched children. Scrooge pities them, but the Ghost quotes his own words to him: 'Are there no prisons . . . no workhouses?'

The Third Spirit is a mysterious, shrouded apparition: the Ghost of Christmas Yet to Come. The repentant Scrooge fears it and begs it for comfort, but it will not speak. It shows him his own death and burial, unmourned, and takes him to the sad Cratchit home, where Tiny Tim is now only a beloved memory. Scrooge, horrified, declares that he is not the man he was, and begs for another chance, promising to honour Christmas in his heart. The Spirit vanishes, and Scrooge finds himself alone in his bedroom.

With dawning joy, he realizes that Time has stood still and that the Spirits have all visited him on the same night,

Scrooge and Bob Cratchit 'keeping Christmas well'

Christmas Eve. It is Christmas Morning now, and he has been given his chance to lead an altered life. He buys a huge turkey and sends it round to the Cratchits', visits his relations and startles them by his change of heart, raises Bob's salary and provides medical help for Tiny Tim, who will not die after all. The Spirits, satisfied, visit him no more.

2. THE CRICKET ON THE HEARTH, a Fairy Tale of Home

John Peerybingle, the Carrier, is a contented man of middle-age with a plump pretty wife and a plump pretty baby; their fireside is enlivened by the singing of a cricket, which is like a fireside fairy to them, and, Dot Peerybingle says, brings them luck. Dot is horrified to learn that John has just collected a wedding-cake for the marriage of Tackleton the Toymaker, a hard and unattractive man, with the beautiful young May Fielding, Dot's one-time schoolfellow. John has also collected a human passenger, a white-haired old stranger who settles comfortably by their hearth. Tackleton calls, and invites them all to the wedding, pointing out grimly that he; like John, is going to take a wife half his age.

Dot goes off to make up a bed for the stranger, and John is puzzled to hear Tilly Slowboy, the nursemaid, talking to the baby about someone whose hair grew brown and curly when its cap was lifted off. He realizes that his wife has been alarmed by something, and connects this with Tilly's mysterious remark.

Next to Tackleton's workshop is the house of Caleb Plummer and his blind daughter, Bertha. Caleb is a good-natured man employed by Tackleton, desperately poor but keeping his poverty from his daughter, whom he kindly deceives with stories of his rich clothes and youthful appearance. Bertha believes Tackleton to be a noble character with an unfortunately gruff manner and rejoices

The Peerybingles at their fireside

that her friend May is going to marry him. But after a party to celebrate the engagement Bertha breaks down and confesses to her father that she loves Tackleton. Caleb realizes that his well-meant deceit has led to the breaking of Bertha's heart.

Bertha and Tackleton react differently to the presence of the old stranger at the Peerybingle house. Bertha is puzzled by something familiar in his step, and Tackleton appears suspicious of him and of Dot's evident agitation in his presence. He shows John, through a window, Dot and the stranger walking together in intimate converse, the stranger transformed to a young man and Dot replacing the white wig on his head. Left alone, John broods by the fire, and the cricket sings to him of his own happy image of his wife and of the strangeness of her apparent infidelity.

Next morning, the stranger has disappeared. Tackleton is disappointed when John tells him that he still loves Dot and only reproaches himself for having expected her to be happy with a husband so much older than herself. It is the wedding-morning of May and Tackleton. Caleb resolves to tell Bertha the truth, that Tackleton is a villain, and that their own home is a poor place. Bertha is shocked and grieved, but recovers and tells Caleb that she is glad to know him as he really is, and that she would rather live with her eyes spiritually open. Dot comforts her with news of a happy surprise and ushers in a young man, the same whom John had seen in her company. It is Edward Plummer, Caleb's son and Bertha's brother, returned from South America, where he fled years before after a quarrel. He had loved May Fielding, and she him; he returned in disguise to see whether or not she had forgotten him. Now he knows that May had thought him dead, and had been about to sacrifice herself to a man she hated, he has revealed himself. John begs Dot to forgive his suspicions, Tackleton is confounded, the wedding called off, and all ends in general rejoicings, as the cricket joins in with its merry chirp.

3. THE CHIMES, a Goblin Story

Beneath the shadow of an old church Toby Veck stands in all weathers, waiting for jobs. Toby (known as 'Trotty' from his gait) is an old ticket-porter, a runner of errands. A weak, spare old man, he is full of energy and cheerfulness, although very poor. Meg, his daughter, brings him his dinner in a basin, and they share it. The chimes of the church, which Trotty loves, ring for their grace. Richard, Meg's sweetheart, a young blacksmith,

Trotty Veck and the Chimes

arrives, and they plan a wedding for the next morning, New Year's Day.

They are turned away from their place on the steps of a grand house by Alderman Cute and Mr. Filer, who blame Trotty for his extravagance in eating tripe. Trotty sadly reflects that the poor can't do right. Alderman Cute forecasts a sordid future for Meg if she and Richard marry. As the gentlemen leave, the chimes seem to say to Trotty, 'Put 'em down! Put 'em down!'—meaning such poor people as himself.

He is sent on an errand to Sir Joseph Bowley's, where he learns that a countryman named Will Fern is to be arrested as a vagabond. On his way home he encounters Fern, carrying his little niece Lilian. They are looking for a friend in London but cannot find her. Trotty takes them home and makes them welcome, he and Meg sacrificing their meagre amount of food to the visitors. After supper Trotty sits reading the newspaper, with its account of the suicide of a desperate young mother, and as he listens to the bells above him he feels they are calling him. He steals out to the church and climbs up to the bell-tower. Its eerie atmosphere overcomes him, and he swoons.

When he regains consciousness he sees that the tower is swarming with goblin figures, the spirits of the bells. They accuse him of having wronged them by hearing in their voices echoes of the world's troubles and sins, and tell him that he has erred in charity. Then they bid him listen and learn. He sees, at the foot of the tower, his own dead body. Then he is taken to Meg's impoverished home, and sees her and Lilian, now a young woman, saddened by their lot. Lilian says she is tempted to lead a wicked life rather than work so cruelly hard.

He is led to Sir Joseph Bowley's, and hears of a suicide in high life, lamented by all, not condemned as the young mother had been condemned. Will Fern enters and makes a revolutionary speech demanding better homes and better food for the poor. Moving on, Trotty sees Meg, even more worn with suffering, and Richard, a moody, drunken sloven. He hears from their talk that Lilian has gone on the streets. Another vision shows him Meg and Richard married, and Richard dying in misery and squalor at the house of Mrs. Chickenstalker, a local tradeswoman, now married to the Bowleys' porter. Meg, alone and desperate, is turned out of her lodgings and cannot find others. She goes to the river with her baby, determined to end her sufferings. Trotty begs the chimes to save her, and says that he has learnt his lesson—he will no longer condemn his own kind, the poor and helpless. If they sin, it is Society which makes them do so. He finds himself holding Meg in his arms—and awakens, to a happy

New Year's morning, with Meg, young, blooming and normal, beside him. The dreadful dream is over and the chimes are ringing in the New Year. Mrs. Chickenstalker appears and proves to be the friend for whom Will Fern was seeking. She welcomes him and Lilian. Meg and Richard prepare for their wedding, joined in their festivities by the neighbours.

4. THE HAUNTED MAN and THE GHOST'S BARGAIN

Redlaw, a melancholy, thoughtful man, is oppressed and haunted by the memory of a wrong he sustained long ago. The ghost of Himself offers him the power of forgetfulness—but he must pass this on to all he meets. He does so, and it destroys everything good in the lives of those about him. Through Milly, an angelically charitable woman, he regains his memory and is able to restore it to others. 'Sorrow, wrong, and trouble . . . should be active with us.'

5. THE BATTLE OF LIFE, A Love Story

Dr. Jeddler has two daughters, Grace and Marion. Their house stands on the site of a great battle of olden times. Marion is engaged to Alfred Heathfield, but knows that her sister loves him, and sacrifices herself by pretending to elope with another man. Six years later she returns to find, as she had wished, Grace married to Alfred; her sacrifice has been justified.

THE POOR RELATION'S STORY

The poor relation, Michael, tells how his adored

Johnny holds the baby while his father opens the shop

Christiana, against all expectations, married him, and made of his home a castle. But at the end of his story he admits that his castle is only in the air.

THE CHILD'S STORY

The parable of a grandfather's life in terms of a traveller who meets a child, who takes him on a magic journey.

THE SCHOOLBOY'S STORY

The story of Old Cheeseman, second Latin master at a boarding-school, whose only friend is Jane, an assistant matron. He comes into a fortune and marries her.

NOBODY'S STORY

A labourer lives and dies, oppressed by Society and blamed for its wrongs. 'The story of Nobody is the story of the rank and file of the earth.'

THE SEVEN POOR TRAVELLERS

At a Rochester lodging-house for Six Poor Travellers, the story-teller hears the tale of Richard Doubledick, Private in a regiment of the line, who has joined the army merely in order to get shot after being jilted. He is redeemed from dissipation by Captain Taunton, who dies in his arms after a battle. He is wounded, finds his love again, and under Taunton's influence forgives his enemies.

THE HOLLY TREE: THREE BRANCHES

A Christmas traveller reflects on Inns, hears the Boots' story of the elopement of two children, Harry and Norah; and learns from the man he thought his rival that his sweetheart Angela is still true to him.

THE WRECK OF THE GOLDEN MARY

Captain Ravender takes on the command of a merchant ship, the *Golden Mary*, bearing among her passengers a little girl whom he calls 'Golden Lucy'. The ship strikes an iceberg and is wrecked. The Captain and passengers escape in boats. For twenty-seven days, during which Lucy dies, they are afloat before rescue.

THE PERILS OF CERTAIN ENGLISH PRISONERS

On the Island of Silver-Store, off the Mosquito Coast, a little English colony mainly consisting of women and children is beset by pirates, and resists nobly. Gill Davis, the story-teller, falls in love with Miss Maryon, a brave young lady, who later becomes his benefactor.

GOING INTO SOCIETY

The tale of Chops, a dwarf in a travelling fair, kind, optimistic and poetic, with a perpetual urge to 'Go into Society'. He gets his wish when he wins a lottery, but is robbed and disillusioned, and returns to his showman friend to die.

THE HAUNTED HOUSE

The author takes a number of friends to occupy a much-haunted house, only to find that its ghost is the spectre of his own innocent childhood.

A MESSAGE FROM THE SEA

Captain Jorgan, an American, brings a message from a sailor thought to be drowned, to his brother. It deals with money left by his father, and said to be stolen. The brother's marriage is threatened by this; he and Jorgan investigate, and find the money actually belongs to the boy's future father-in-law. The sailor supposed drowned proves to be alive and returns to make his wife and small daughter happy.

Tom Tiddler's Ground

A discursion about the visit of a traveller to a hermit, with whom he reasons, telling him he should abandon his lonely and dirty state. He introduces Miss Killy Kimmeens, a little girl left alone in a boarding-school for the day, who has come to him for help. They abandon the hermit to his chosen life.

Somebody's Luggage

A head waiter steals some manuscripts from the luggage of a traveller, and sends them to *All The Year Round*: first the story of an Englishman in France, who takes pity on an orphan child; then of a jealous man who loses his sweetheart to a pavement artist. The author, a frustrated journalist, comes back and is delighted to find his stories in print.

Mrs. Lirriper's Lodgings

Mrs. Lirriper, a London lodging-house keeper, takes in a young couple called Edson. The supposed husband deserts the girl, who is expecting a child. She dies in giving birth to it, and Mrs. Lirriper brings up the boy, Jemmy, with the help of her friend and lodger, Major Jackman.

Mrs. Lirriper's Legacy

Mrs. Lirriper hears that an unknown Englishman who is dying in France wishes to leave her a legacy. She goes to him, accompanied by Jemmy and Major Jackman, and finds that he is Jemmy's father, dying repentant. Jemmy is kept in ignorance of his background, and invents a romantic version of it, which Mrs. Lirriper allows him to believe.

DOCTOR MARIGOLD

Doctor Marigold, a travelling showman, loses his daughter Sophy, who has been maltreated by her mother. His wife later commits suicide. He adopts a deaf-and-dumb girl, brings her up as his daughter, and sends her to be educated, with great success. His adopted daughter marries a deaf-and-dumb husband, they go to China for five years, and return with their child, who is the image of her mother but can both speak and hear. An interlude in Dr. Marigold's story, called 'To be taken with a pinch of Salt', tells of a man who had a vision of two men unknown to him, who proved to be murderer and victim in a murder trial for which he was Foreman of the Jury.

MUGBY JUNCTION

A discontented traveller, Young Jackson, known as Barbox Brothers, from the name on his luggage, arrives at Mugby Junction. He meets Phoebe, invalid daughter of 'Lamps', and is shamed by her brightness and resignation to her fate. In another town he encounters Polly, the child of his old love, and is reconciled with her parents. The Boy at Mugby Junction talks of his life. The Story of the Signalman is told; after three spectral warnings of danger, he is killed by an engine.

MINOR STORIES

NO THOROUGHFARE

Walter Wilding, the young head of a firm of London wine-merchants, reveres the memory of his mother, who took him as a child from the Foundling Hospital, where she had left him in infancy. He is horrified to discover that she had taken the wrong child; and he begins a search for the real Walter Wilding, but dies before he can pursue it far.

His partner, George Vendale, falls in love with Marguerite Obenreizer, niece of Jules Obenreizer, traveller for a Swiss wine firm. Obenreizer, who has himself designs on Marguerite, tells Vendale to double his income before he thinks of proposing to her. Vendale and Obenreizer travel to Switzerland together. On the journey Obenreizer makes an abortive attempt on Vendale's life, and later succeeds in pushing him over a precipice. He clings there until rescued by Marguerite, whose suspicions of Obenreizer had been aroused. Obenreizer is unmasked as an embezzler and would-be murderer, and the true Walter Wilding is found in the person of Vendale.

THE LAZY TOUR OF TWO IDLE APPRENTICES

Thomas Idle and Francis Goodchild take a journey to the North of England. They take note of the natives they meet, hear strange stories at Doncaster and Lancaster, visit a lunatic asylum, and attend the Doncaster Races.

MASTER HUMPHREY'S CLOCK

Old Master Humphrey, from the chimney-corner of his ancient London house, tells how he, a deaf gentleman, and two other friends, Jack Redburn and Owen Miles, beguile a night a week by the telling of tales. The manuscripts of these are stored in Master Humphrey's grandfather clock.

The clock case's first manuscript introduces Gog and Magog, the Guildhall giants, and a story of Elizabethan days dealing with Hugh Graham, apprentice to a bowyer, who revenged himself upon his sweetheart's seducer.

Its second story tells of an uncle who hated his nephew, murdered the child and buried its body, and was brought to justice by conscience.

Mr. Pickwick calls, presents himself as a candidate for Master Humphrey's story-telling circle, and tells a tale of suspected witchcraft in Windsor during the reign of James the First.

Mr. Pickwick is followed to Master Humphrey's house by Sam Weller and old Tony Weller, who relates anecdotes of his two-year-old grandson. Sam Weller forms a story-telling club below stairs, which includes Master Humphrey's barber, to whom he relates a tale of a hairdresser in love with his female dummy.

Tony Weller brings his grandson to meet Master Humphrey's housekeeper, for whom he has a certain *tendresse*.

Master Humphrey, after the death of the Deaf Gentleman, reflects on his own lonely life, now that his best friend is dead and his clock has stopped for ever.

HUNTED DOWN

Mr. Sampson, Chief Manager of a Life Assurance Office, meets and takes an instant dislike to Julius Slinkton, of the Middle Temple. Slinkton tells him that one of his two beloved nieces has just died, and that the remaining one is delicate. He asks Sampson to effect an insurance policy for a friend, Beckwith. Some months later Sampson meets him and his niece, Miss Niner, at Scarborough. She tells him of an invalid gentleman in a wheel-chair who seems to follow her about. Sampson encounters her 'shadow', talks to him, and returns to say that he is an old acquaintance. Miss Niner confides to Sampson, in her uncle's absence, that she feels herself to be dying, as her sister died. Sampson warns her that she must at once go away with the old gentleman in the wheel-chair, if she is to save herself.

Slinkton reproaches Sampson with having lured her away; but Sampson has been working with the man calling himself Beckwith, really the lover of the dead niece, who has laid a careful trap for Slinkton by pretending to be taken in by him, and who was the 'invalid' in the wheel-chair. He accuses Slinkton of murder, and Slinkton takes poison and dies. Miss Niner survives to marry Sampson's nephew.

HOLIDAY ROMANCE

William Tinkling, aged eight, his small bride Nettie Ashford, and their friends Robert and Alice decide on a plan to educate the grown-ups, who are lacking in imagination. Alice tells the story of the Magic Fishbone. Robert tells the piratical tale of Captain Boldheart, who kidnaps his bride while she is bathing at Margate. Nettie tells of Mrs. Orange and Mrs. Lemon, children taking the place of grown-ups, who entertain the troublesome grown-ups, now transformed to children. It is decided that Mrs. Lemon shall have them with her for the holidays, and that they shall altogether be kept in their proper place.

GEORGE SILVERMAN'S EXPLANATION

George Silverman is brought up in a squalid cellar in Preston. His parents die of alcoholism and fever, and he is taken away to be educated by Brother Hawkyard, of a Nonconformist sect. The boy grows up afraid of infecting others with fever, and gains a reputation for being morose. He wins a scholarship, goes to college, and becomes a clergyman. He obtains a living through the patronage of Lady Fareway, who presses him into service as her secretary. George falls in love with his pupil, Lady Fareway's daughter Adelina, and she with him, but he considers himself too humble to marry her. He introduces her to another pupil, Granville, with the deliberate intention of their being attracted to each other. His plan succeeds, and they are married, George performing the ceremony. Lady Fareway accuses George of having brought about the match to get money out of Granville, and demands that he resigns his living. For some years he suffers from her vengeful pursuit, but finally reaches a peaceful spot wherein to spend the remainder of his life.

A SAMPLER OF QUOTATIONS

A SAMPLER OF QUOTATIONS

SUCH IS LIFE

It is a melancholy truth that even great men have their poor relations.—*Bleak House*.

'Never have a mission, my dear child.'—Mr. Jellyby, *Bleak House*.

'Experentia does it—as papa used to say.'—Mrs. Micawber, *David Copperfield*.

'Annual income twenty pounds, annual expenditure nineteen nineteen six, result happiness. Annual income twenty pounds, annual expenditure twenty pounds ought and six, result misery.'—Mr. Micawber, *David Copperfield*.

'It was as true,' said Mr. Barkis, 'as taxes is. And nothing's truer than them.'—*David Copperfield*.

'On the Rampage, Pip, and off the Rampage, Pip; such is Life!'—Joe Gargery, *Great Expectations*.

'Oh Sairey, Sairey, little do we know wot lays afore us!'—Mrs. Gamp, *Martin Chuzzlewit*.

'Subdue your appetites, my dears, and you've conquered human natur.'—Mr. Squeers, *Nicholas Nickleby*.

There is a passion for hunting something deeply implanted in the human breast.—*Oliver Twist*.

'It's always best on these occasions to do what the mob do.'

'But suppose there are two mobs,' suggested Mr. Snodgrass.

'Shout with the largest,' replied Mr. Pickwick.—*The Pickwick Papers*.

'It's over and can't be helped, and that's one consolation, as they always say in Turkey, ven they cuts the wrong man's head off.'—Sam Weller, *The Pickwick Papers*.

'The have-his-carcase, next to the perpetual motion, is vun of the blessedest things as wos ever made.'—Sam Weller, *The Pickwick Papers*.

'Vell, gov'ner, ve must all come to it, one day or another.'

'So we must, Sammy,' said Mr. Weller the elder.

'There's a Providence in it all,' said Sam.

'O' course there is,' replied his father with a nod of grave approval. 'Wot 'ud become of the undertakers vithout it, Sammy?'—*The Pickwick Papers*.

'Anythin' for a quiet life, as the man said wen he took the sitivation at the lighthouse.'—Sam Weller, *The Pickwick Papers*.

'What a world of gammon and spinnage it is, though, ain't it!'—Miss Mowcher, *David Copperfield*.

'Any man may be in good spirits and good temper when he's well dressed. There ain't much credit in that.'—Mark Tapley, *Martin Chuzzlewit*.

'Mind and matter,' said the lady in the wig, 'glide swift into the vortex of immensity. Howls the sublime, and softly sleeps the calm Ideal, in the whispering chambers of Imagination.'—*Martin Chuzzlewit*.

'Some people may be Rooshans, and others may be Prooshans; they are born so and will please themselves. Them which is of other naturs thinks different.'—Mrs. Gamp, *Martin Chuzzlewit*.

In love of home the love of country has its rise.—*The Old Curiosity Shop*.

'She'll vish there wos more, and that's the great art o' letter writin'.'—Sam Weller, *The Pickwick Papers*.

'My advice is, never do tomorrow what you can do today.'—Mr. Micawber, *David Copperfield*.

'We must meet reverses boldly . . . we must live misfortune down.'—Betsey Trotwood, *David Copperfield*.

There are dark shadows on the earth, but its lights are stronger in the contrast.—*The Pickwick Papers*.

'Let us be moral. Let us contemplate existence.'—Mr. Pecksniff, *Martin Chuzzlewit*.

'How common the saying "The morning's too fine to last!" How well it might be applied to our everyday existence!'—The Dismal Man, *The Pickwick Papers*.

'Some conjurers say that number three is the magic number, and some say number seven. It's neither, my friend, neither. It's number one.'—Fagin, *Oliver Twist*.

There are very few moments in a man's existence when he experiences so much ludicrous distress, or meets with so little charitable commiseration, as when he is in pursuit of his own hat.—*The Pickwick Papers*.

Certain it is that minds, like bodies, will often fall into a pimpled ill-conditioned state from mere excess of comfort, and like them, are often successfully cured by remedies in themselves very nauseous and unpalatable.—*Barnaby Rudge*.

It is when our budding hopes are nipped beyond recovery by some rough wind, that we are the most disposed to picture to ourselves what flowers they might have borne.—*Dombey and Son*.

'More domestic unhappiness has come of easy fainting, Doll, than from all the greater passions put together.'
—Gabriel Varden, *Barnaby Rudge*.

'She's a rum 'un is Natur . . . Natur is more easier conceived than described.'—Squeers, *Nicholas Nickleby*.

'Say, like those wicked Turks, there is no What's-his-name but Thingummy, and What-you-may-call-it is his prophet!'—Mrs. Skewton, *Dombey and Son*.

'Once a gentleman, and always a gentleman.'—Rigaud, *Little Dorrit*.

'It was a maxim with Foxey—our revered father, gentlemen—"Always suspect everybody".'—Sampson Brass, *The Old Curiosity Shop*.

'Here's the rule for bargains: "Do other men, for they would do you." That's the true business precept.'—Jonas Chuzzlewit, *Martin Chuzzlewit*.

Breakings up are capital things in our school days, but in after life they are painful enough—*The Pickwick Papers*.

Our whole life . . . is a story more or less intelligible,—generally less; but we shall read it by a clearer light when it is ended.—The Seven Poor Travellers, *Christmas Stories*.

'If Natur has gifted a man with powers of argeyment, a man has a right to make the best of 'em, and has not a right to stand on false delicacy, and deny that he is so gifted; for that is a turning of his back on Natur, a flouting of her, a slighting of her precious caskets, and a proving of one's self to be a swine that isn't worth her scattering pearls before.'—John Willet, *Barnaby Rudge*.

Everything in our lives, whether of good or evil, affects us most by contrast.—*The Old Curiosity Shop*.

'Never . . . be mean in anything, never be false; never be cruel. Avoid those three vices, Trot, and I can always be hopeful of you.'—Betsey Trotwood, *David Copperfield*.

I wonder that the great master who knew everything, when he called Sleep the death of each day's life, did not call Dreams the insanity of each day's sanity.—*The Uncommercial Traveller*.

THE TENDER PASSION

'I positively adore Miss Dombey; —I—I am perfectly sore with loving her.'—Mr. Toots, *Dombey and Son*.

'If you could see my legs when I take my boots off, you'd form some idea of what unrequited affection is.'—Mr. Toots, *Dombey and Son*.

'When the choristers chaunt, I hear Miss Shepherd. In the service I mentally insert Miss Shepherd's name; I put her in among the Royal Family. At home, in my own room, I am sometimes moved to cry out, "Oh, Miss Shepherd!" in a transport of love.'—David Copperfield, *David Copperfield*.

'The eldest Miss Larkins is not a chicken; for the youngest Miss Larkins is not that, and the eldest must be three or four years older. Perhaps the eldest Miss Larkins may be about thirty. My passion for her is beyond all bounds.'—David Copperfield, *David Copperfield*.

'She was more than human to me. She was a Fairy, a Sylph, I don't know what she was—anything that no one ever saw, and everything that everybody ever wanted.' —David Copperfield, *David Copperfield*.

'Darling, I dare propose to you. Stop there. If it be bad to idolize you, I am the worst of men; if it be good, I am the best.'—John Jasper, *Edwin Drood*.

"'Twas ever thus—from childhood's hour I've seen my fondest hopes decay, I never loved a tree or flower but 'twas the first to fade away; I never nursed a dear Gazelle, to glad me with its soft black eye, but when it came to know me well, and love me, it was sure to marry a market-gardener.'—Dick Swiveller, *The Old Curiosity Shop*.

Joe was clean out of his senses . . . not to say over head and ears, but over the Monument and the top of Saint Paul's in love.—*Barnaby Rudge*.

'For you, and for any dear to you, I would do anything. Try to hold me in your mind, at some quiet times, as ardent and sincere in this one thing.'—Sydney Carton, *A Tale of Two Cities*.

. . . a highly coloured representation of a couple of human hearts skewered together with an arrow, cooking before a cheerful fire, while a male and female cannibal in modern attire . . . were approaching the meal with hungry eyes, up a serpentine gravel path leading thereunto. A decidedly indelicate young gentleman, in a pair of wings and nothing else, was depicted as superintending the cooking . . . and the whole formed a 'valentine.'—*The Pickwick Papers*.

'So I take the privilidge of the day, Mary, my dear—as the gen'lm'n in difficulties did, wen he valked out of a Sunday,—to tell you that the first and only time I see you, your likeness was took on my hart in much quicker time and brighter colours than ever a likeness was took by the profeel macheen.'—Sam Weller, *The Pickwick Papers*.

'Here lie the mortal remains of JOHN CHIVERY, Never anything worth mentioning, Who died about the end of the year one thousand eight hundred and twenty-six, Of a broken heart, Requesting with his last breath that the word AMY might be inscribed over his ashes, Which was accordingly directed to be done, By his afflicted Parents.' —*Little Dorrit*.

'I kissed her cheek as she turned it to me. I think I would have gone through a great deal to kiss her cheek. But I felt that the kiss was given to the coarse common boy as a piece of money might have been, and that it was worth nothing.'—Pip, *Great Expectations*.

Mystery and disappointment are not absolutely indispensable to the growth of love, but they are very often its powerful auxiliaries.—*Nicholas Nickleby*.

'Will you permit me, fairest creature, to ask you one question, in the absence of the planet Venus, who has gone on business to the Horse Guards, and would otherwise— jealous of your superior charms—interpose between us?' —The Gentleman in Small-clothes, *Nicholas Nickleby.*

'Be mine, be mine . . . Gog and Magog, Gog and Magog. Be mine!'—The Gentleman in Small-clothes, *Nicholas Nickleby.*

Boots could assure me that it was 'better than a picter, and equal to a play, to see them babies, with their long, bright curling hair, their sparkling eyes, and their beautiful light tread, a rambling about the garden, deep in love.' —*The Holly Tree.*

'Lower me down to him,' she said . . . 'or I will dash myself to pieces! I am a peasant, and I know no giddiness or fear; and this is nothing to me, and I passionately love him. Lower me down!'—Marguerite Obenreizer, *No Thoroughfare.*

'My dear Martin,' said Mary.
'My dear Mary,' said Martin; and lovers are such a singular kind of people, that this is all they did say just then.—*Martin Chuzzlewit.*

'I have seen him, again and again, sitting over his pie at dinner with his spoon a perfect fixture in his mouth, looking at your sister. I have seen him standing in a corner of our drawing-room, gazing at her, in such a lonely, melancholy state, that he was more like a Pump than a man, and might have drawed tears.'—Mrs. Todgers, *Martin Chuzzlewit.*

'Oh, Mr. Woodcourt . . . it is a great thing to win love, it is a great thing to win love!'—Esther Summerson, *Bleak House.*

'I'll tell thee how the maiden wept, Mrs. Boffin,
When her true love was slain, ma'am,
And how her broken spirit slept, Mrs. Boffin,
And never woke again, ma'am.
I'll tell thee (If agreeable to Mr. Boffin) how the steed
    drew nigh,
And left his lord afar;
And if my tale (which I hope Mr. Boffin might excuse)
    should make you sigh,
I'll strike the light guitar.'—Silas Wegg, *Our Mutual
Friend.*

'A young gentleman may be over-careful of himself, or
he may be under-careful of himself. He may brush his hair
too regular, or too unregular. He may wear his boots much
too large for him, or much too small. That is according as
the young gentleman has his original character formed. But
let him go to which extreme he may, sir, there's a young
lady in both of 'em.'—Mrs. Crupp, *David Copperfield.*

Matrimony is proverbially a serious undertaking. Like
an overweening predilection for brandy-and-water, it is a
misfortune into which a man easily falls, and from which he
finds it remarkably difficult to extricate himself.—*Sketches
by Boz.*

A wedding is a licensed subject to joke upon, but there
really is no great joke in the matter after all.—*The
Pickwick Papers.*

'I read in th' papers every 'Sizes, every Sessions . . . how
th' supposed unpossibility o' ever getting unchained from
one another, at any price, on any terms, brings blood upon
this land, and brings many common married fok to battle,
murder, and sudden death.'—Stephen Blackpool, *Hard
Times.*

LONDON PARTICULAR

It is strange with how little notice, good, bad or indifferent, a man may live and die in London.—*Sketches by Boz.*

Of the numerous receptacles for misery and distress with which the streets of London unhappily abound, there are, perhaps, none which present such striking scenes as the pawnbrokers' shops.—*Sketches by Boz.*

You look down the long perspective of Oxford-street, the gas-lights mournfully reflected on the wet pavement, and can discern no speck in the road to encourage the belief that there is a cab or a coach to be had.—*Sketches by Boz.*

If the Parks be 'the lungs of London', we wonder what Greenwich Fair is.—*Sketches by Boz.*

If the regular City man, who leaves Lloyd's at five o'clock and drives home to Hackney, Clapton, Stamford-hill, or elsewhere, can be said to have any daily recreation beyond his dinner, it is his garden.—*Sketches by Boz.*

And what is Scotland-yard now? How have its old customs changed; and how has the ancient simplicity of its inhabitants faded away!—*Sketches by Boz.*

What inexhaustible food for speculation do the streets of London afford!—*Sketches by Boz.*

The appearance presented by the streets of London an hour before sunrise, on a summer's morning, is most striking . . . but the streets of London, to be beheld in the very height of their glory, should be seen on a dark, dull, murky winter's night, when there is just enough damp gently stealing down to make the pavement greasy . . . —*Sketches by Boz*.

A dirtier or more wretched place [Oliver] had never seen. The street was very narrow and muddy, and the air was impregnated with filthy odours. There were a good many small shops; but the only stock in trade appeared to be heaps of children.—*Oliver Twist*.

Suddenly, [Sikes] took the desperate resolution of going back to London. 'There's somebody to speak to there, at all events,' he thought. 'A good hiding-place, too.'—*Oliver Twist*.

'We drove through the dirtiest and darkest streets that ever were seen in the world (I thought), and in such a distracting state of confusion that I wondered how the people kept their senses, until we passed into sudden quietude under an old gateway.'—Esther Summerson, *Bleak House*.

'This is about a London particular *now*, ain't it, miss?' . . .
'The fog is very dense, indeed!' said I.—Mr. Guppy and Esther Summerson.—*Bleak House*.

London is shabby in contrast with Edinburgh, with Aberdeen, with Exeter, with Liverpool, with a bright little town like Bury St. Edmunds . . . in detail, one would say it can rarely fail to be a disappointing piece of shabbiness to a stranger from any of those places. There is nothing shabbier than Drury Lane, in Rome itself.—*The Uncommercial Traveller*.

It was a foggy night in London, and the fog was heavy and dark. Animate London, with smarting eyes and irritated lungs, was blinking, wheezing, and choking; inanimate London was a sooty spectre, divided in purpose between being visible and invisible and so being wholly neither.—*Our Mutual Friend*.

Fifty thousand lairs surrounded him where people lived so unwholesomely, that fair water put into their crowded rooms on Saturday night, would be corrupt on Sunday morning . . . through the heart of the town a deadly sewer ebbed and flowed, in the place of a fine fresh river.—*Little Dorrit*.

Down by the Docks they eat the largest oysters and scatter the roughest oyster shells known to the descendants of Saint George and the Dragon.—*The Uncommercial Traveller*.

There was a dense brown fog in Piccadilly, and it became positively black and in the last degree oppressive East of Temple Bar.—*Doctor Marigold*.

'Have you seen anything of London, yet?' . . .
'Why, yes, Sir—but we didn't find that it come up to its likeness in the red bills—it is there drawd too archictoo-ralooral.'—Herbert Pocket and Joe Gargery, *Great Expectations*.

It was a Sunday evening in London, gloomy, close and stale. Maddening church bells of all degrees of dissonance, sharp and flat, cracked and clear, fast and slow, made the brick-and-mortar echoes hideous . . . in every thorough-fare, up almost every alley, and down almost every turning, some doleful bell was throbbing, jerking, tolling, as if the Plague were in the city and the dead-carts were going round.—*Little Dorrit*.

. . . there he sits, munching and gnawing, and looking up at the great Cross on the summit of St. Paul's Cathedral, glittering above a red and violet-tinted cloud of smoke. From the boy's face one might suppose that sacred emblem to be, in his eyes, the crowning confusion of that great, confused city.—*Bleak House*.

Even on this stranger's wilderness of London there is some rest. Its steeples and towers, and its one great dome, grow more ethereal; its smoky housetops lose their grossness, in the pale effulgence; the noises that arise from the streets are fewer and are softened and the footsteps on the pavements pass more tranquilly away.—*Bleak House*.

Being in a humour for complete solitude and uninterrupted meditation this autumn, I have taken a lodging for six weeks in the most unfrequented part of England—in a word, in London.—*The Uncommercial Traveller*.

They [the City churches] are worth a Sunday-exploration, now and then, for they yet echo, not unharmoniously, to the time when the City of London really was London.—*The Uncommercial Traveller*.

Life and death went hand in hand; wealth and poverty stood side by side; repletion and starvation laid them down together. But it was London.—*Nicholas Nickleby*.

LEGAL JUDGMENTS

'I expect a judgment. Shortly. On the Day of Judgment.' —Miss Flite, *Bleak House*.

'Keep out of Chancery . . . it's being ground to bits in a slow mill; it's being roasted at a slow fire; it's being stung to death by single bees; it's being drowned by drops; it's going mad by grains.'—Tom Jarndyce, *Bleak House.*

'Everybody must have copies, over and over again, of everything that has accumulated about it in the way of cartloads of papers . . . and must go down the middle and up again, through such an infernal country-dance of costs and fees and nonsense and corruption, as was never dreamed of in the wildest visions of a witch's Sabbath.' —John Jarndyce, *Bleak House.*

Mr. Tulkinghorn is not in a common way. He wants no clerks. He is a great reservoir of confidences, not to be so tapped . . . His clients want *him*; he is all in all.—*Bleak House.*

. . . the general crowd, in whose way the forensic wisdom of ages has interposed a million of obstacles to the transaction of the commonest business of life.—*Bleak House.*

It is the long vacation in the regions of Chancery Lane. The good ships Law and Equity, those teak-built, copper-bottomed, iron-fastened, brazen-faced, and not by any means fast-sailing Clippers, are laid up in ordinary.—*Bleak House.*

To see everything going on so smoothly, and to think of the roughness of the suitors' lives and deaths; to see all that full dress and ceremony, and to think of the waste, and want, and beggared misery it represented . . . —*Bleak House.*

'When those learned gentlemen begin to raise moss-roses from the powder they sow in their wigs, I shall begin to be astonished too!'—John Jarndyce, *Bleak House.*

'I said, sir, that of all the disgraceful and rascally proceedings that ever were attempted, this is the most so. I repeat it, sir.'

'You hear that, Mr. Wicks?' said Dodson.

'You won't forget these expressions, Mr. Jackson?' said Fogg.

'Perhaps you would like to call us swindlers, sir,' said Dodson. 'Pray do, sir, if you feel disposed; now pray do, sir.'

'I do,' said Mr. Pickwick. 'You *are* swindlers.'—*The Pickwick Papers*.

'You know, my dear sir, if you *will* take the management of your affairs into your own hands after intrusting them to your solicitor, you must also take the consequences.'—Mr. Perker, *The Pickwick Papers*.

'Gentlemen of your profession, sir,' said Mr. Pickwick, 'see the worst side of human nature. All its disputes, all its ill-will and bad blood, rise up before you.'—*The Pickwick Papers*.

'Why, I don't exactly know about perjury, my dear sir . . . harsh word, my dear sir, very harsh word indeed. It's a legal fiction, my dear sir, nothing more.'—Mr. Perker, *The Pickwick Papers*.

'It's very unpleasant keepin' us vaitin' here. I'd ha' got half a dozen have-his-carcases ready, pack'd up and all, by this time.'—Sam Weller, *The Pickwick Papers*.

There is a box of barristers on their right hand; there is an inclosure of insolvent debtors on their left; and there is an inclined plane of most especially dirty faces in their front. These gentlemen are the Commissioners of the Insolvent Court.—*The Pickwick Papers*.

'This is the Marshalsea, sir.'

'The debtors' prison? . . . Can any one go in here?'

'Anyone can *go in*,' said the old man; plainly adding by the significance of his emphasis, 'but it is not every one who can go out.'—Arthur Clennam and Frederick Dorrit, *Little Dorrit.*

'I can understand what you tell me, so very much better than what I read in law-writings.'—Rosa Bud, *Edwin Drood.*

Behind the most ancient part of Holborn, London . . . is a little nook composed of two irregular quadrangles, called Staple Inn . . . It is one of those nooks where a few smoky sparrows twitter in smoky trees, as though they called to one another 'Let us play at country' . . . Moreover, it is one of those nooks which are legal nooks.—*Edwin Drood.*

Conveyancing and he had made such a very indifferent marriage of it that they had separated by consent—if there can be said to be separation where there has never been coming together.—*Edwin Drood.*

'The arm of the law is a strong arm, and a long arm. That is the way I put it.'—Mr. Sapsea, *Edwin Drood.*

'How do you propose to deal with the case, sir?' enquired the clerk in a low voice.

'Summarily,' replied Mr. Fang. 'He stands committed for three months—hard labour of course. Clear the office.'

The door was opened for this purpose, and a couple of men were preparing to carry the insensible boy to his cell . . . —*Oliver Twist.*

Within such walls [Metropolitan police offices] enough fantastic tricks are daily played to make the angels blind with weeping.—*Oliver Twist.*

'In other words, you, a lawyer, are here to represent an infraction of the law.'

'Admirably put!' said Bintrey. 'If all the people I have to deal with were only like you, what an easy profession mine would be!'—*No Thoroughfare*.

The magistrates shivered under a single bite of [Jaggers'] finger. Thieves and thieftakers hung in dread rapture on his words, and shrank when a hair of his eyebrows turned in their direction.—*Great Expectations*.

'It's hard in the law to spile a man, I think. It's hard enough to kill him, but it's very hard to spile him, sir.'

'Not at all,' returned the ancient clerk. 'Speak well of the law. Take care of your chest and voice, my good friend, and leave the law to take care of itself.'—Jerry Cruncher and the Clerk, *A Tale of Two Cities*.

We are not by any means devout believers in the old Bow Street Police. To say the truth, we think there was a vast amount of humbug about those worthies.—The Detective Police, *Reprinted Pieces*.

We know that on the only occasion of an offender, liable by the law to death, being brought before Him for His judgment, it was *not* death. We know that He said, 'Thou shalt not kill.' And if we are still to inflict capital punishment because of the Mosaic law . . . it would be equally reasonable to establish the lawfulness of a plurality of wives on the same authority.—Capital Punishment, *Miscellaneous Papers*.

'How many vain pleaders for mercy, do you think have turned away heartsick from the lawyer's office, to find a resting-place in the Thames, or a refuge in the gaol?' —Jack Bamber, *The Pickwick Papers*.

'As a friend of mine used to say to me, "What is there in chambers, in particular?"

"Queer old places," said I.

"Not at all," said he.

"Lonely," said I.

"Not a bit of it," said he. He died one morning of apoplexy, as he was going to open his outer door. Fell with his head in his own letter-box, and there he lay for eighteen months. Everybody thought he'd gone out of town.'

'And how was he found at last?' enquired Mr. Pickwick.

'The benchers determined to have his door broken open, as he hadn't paid any rent for two years. So they did. Forced the lock, and a very dusty skeleton in a blue coat, black knee-shorts, and silks, fell forward, in the arms of the porter who opened the door. Queer, that. Rather, perhaps?'—Jack Bamber, *The Pickwick Papers*.

These sequestered nooks are the public offices of the legal profession, where writs are issued, judgments signed, declarations filed, and numerous other ingenious machines put in motion for the torture and torment of His Majesty's liege subjects, and the comfort and emolument of the practitioners of the law.—*The Pickwick Papers*.

I look upon Gray's Inn generally as one of the most depressing institutions in brick and mortar, known to the children of men.—*The Uncommercial Traveller*.

THE RICH AND THE POOR

'The fact is,' said Mr. Brogley, 'there's a little payment on a bond debt—three hundred and seventy odd, over due; and I'm in possession.'—*Dombey and Son*.

Poverty has its whims and shows of taste, as wealth has.—*Barnaby Rudge*.

If ever household affections and loves are graceful things, they are graceful to the poor.—*The Old Curiosity Shop*.

'Mary,' said the Blind Girl, 'tell me what my home is— what it truly is.'

'It is a poor place, Bertha; very poor and bare indeed. The house will scarcely keep out wind and rain another winter. It is as roughly shielded from the weather, Bertha . . . as your poor father in his sackcloth coat.'—*The Cricket on the Hearth*.

'A few of us are endeavouring to raise a fund to buy the Poor some meat and drink, and means of warmth. We choose this time, because it is a time, of all others, when Want is keenly felt, and Abundance rejoices. What shall I put you down for?'

'Nothing!' Scrooge replied.—*A Christmas Carol*.

Think of that! Bob had but fifteen 'Bob' a week himself; he pocketed on Saturdays but fifteen copies of his Christian name.—*A Christmas Carol*.

From the foldings of its robe it brought two children— wretched, abject, frightful, hideous, miserable . . .

'Spirit! Are they yours?' Scrooge could say no more.

'They are Man's,' said the Spirit, looking down upon them. 'And they cling to me, appealing from their fathers. This boy is Ignorance. This girl is Want.'—*A Christmas Carol*.

'There's a great deal of nonsense talked about Want— "hard up", you know: that's the phrase, isn't it? ha! ha! ha! —and I intend to Put it Down. There's a certain amount of cant in vogue about Starvation, and I mean to Put it Down. That's all.'—Alderman Cute, *The Chimes*.

'He's going to die here, after all. Going to die upon the premises. Going to die in our house!'

'And where should he have died, Tugby?' cried his wife.

'In the workhouse,' he returned. 'What are workhouses made for?'—*The Chimes*.

'I know that our Inheritance is held in store for us by Time. I know that there is a sea of Time to rise one day, before which all who wrong us or oppress us will be swept away like leaves.'—Trotty Veck, *The Chimes*.

'There is not a father,' said the Phantom, 'by whose side, in his daily or nightly walk, these creatures pass; there is not a mother among all the ranks of loving mothers in this land; there is no one risen from the state of childhood, but shall be responsible in his or her degree for this enormity.'
—*The Haunted Man*.

Jo lives—that is to say, Jo has not yet died—in a ruinous place, known to the like of him by the name of Tom-all-Alone's. It is a black, dilapidated street, avoided by all decent people . . . these ruined shelters have bred a crowd of foul existence that crawls in and out of gaps in walls and boards . . . sowing more evil in its every foot-print than Lord Coodle, and Sir Thomas Doodle, and the Duke of Foodle, and all the fine gentlemen in office, down to Zoodle, shall set right in five hundred years.—*Bleak House*.

'Is my daughter a-washin'? Yes, she *is* a washin'. Look at the water. Smell it! That's wot we drinks. How do you like it, and what do you think of gin, instead? An't my place dirty? Yes, it *is* dirty—it's nat'rally dirty, and it's nat'rally onwholesome; and we've had five dirty and onwholesome children, as is all dead infants, and so much the better for them, and for us besides.'—The Brickmaker, *Bleak House*.

So poor a clerk, through having a limited salary, and unlimited family, that he never yet attained the modest object of his ambition; which was, to wear a complete new suit of clothes, hat and boots included, at one time.—*Our Mutual Friend*.

Mr. and Mrs. Veneering were bran-new people in a bran-new house in a bran-new quarter of London. Everything about the Veneerings was spick and span new. All their furniture was new, all their friends were new . . . and if they had set up a great-grandfather, he would have come home in matting from the Pantechnicon, without a scratch upon him, French polished to the crown of his head.—*Our Mutual Friend*.

'You dislike the mention of [the Poor-house]?' said the Secretary.

'Dislike the mention of it?' answered the old woman. 'Kill me sooner than take me there. Throw this pretty child under carthorses' feet and a loaded wagon, sooner than take him there. Come to us and find us all a-dying, and set a light to us all where we lie, and let us all blaze away with the house into a heap of cinders, sooner than move a corpse of us there!'—*Our Mutual Friend*.

'I tell you I am not rich,' repeated Mr. Boffin, 'and I won't have it.'

'You are not rich, sir?' repeated the Secretary, in measured words.

'Well,' returned Mr. Boffin, 'if I am, that's my business. I am not going to spend at this rate, to please you, or anybody. You wouldn't like it, if it was your money . . . Did you ever hear of Daniel Dancer?'

'Another miser? Yes.'

'He was a good 'un,' said Mr. Boffin, 'and he had a sister worthy of him. They never called themselves rich neither. If they *had* called themselves rich, most likely they wouldn't have been so.'—*Our Mutual Friend.*

It took four men, all four a-blaze with gorgeous decoration, and the Chief of them unable to exist with fewer than two gold watches in his pocket, emulative of the noble and chaste fashion set by Monseigneur, to conduct the happy chocolate to Monseigneur's lips . . . Deep would have been the blot upon his escutcheon if his chocolate had been ignobly waited on by only three men; he must have died of two.—*A Tale of Two Cities.*

'Foulon, who told my old father that he might eat grass, when I had no bread to give him! Foulon, who told my baby it might suck grass, when these breasts were dry with want! O mother of God, this Foulon! O Heaven our suffering!'—A Parisienne, *A Tale of Two Cities.*

'When a man tells me anything about imaginative qualities, I always tell that man, whoever he is, that I know what he means. He means turtle soup and venison, with a gold spoon, and that he wants to be set up with a coach and six.'—Bounderby, *Hard Times.*

'With the exception of the heel of Dutch cheese—which is not adapted to the wants of a young family,'—said Mrs. Micawber, 'there is really not a scrap of anything in the larder. I was accustomed to speak of the larder when I lived with papa and mama, and I use the word almost unconsciously. What I mean to express is, that there is nothing to eat in the house.'—*David Copperfield.*

'It's a very remarkable circumstance, sir . . . that poverty and oysters always seems to go together.'—Sam Weller, *The Pickwick Papers.*

THE TIMELY INN

'Good house—nice beds.' The Bull at Rochester. —Jingle, *The Pickwick Papers.*

In the Borough especially, there still remain some half dozen old inns . . . great, rambling, queer old places they are, with galleries, and passages and staircases, wide enough and antiquated enough to furnish materials for a hundred ghost stories.—*The Pickwick Papers.*

The Great White Horse is famous in the neighbourhood, in the same degree as a prize ox, or county paper-chronicled turnip, or unwieldy pig—for its enormous size.—*The Pickwick Papers.*

'I say, old boy, where do you hang out?'
Mr. Pickwick replied that he was at present suspended at the George and Vulture.—*The Pickwick Papers.*

'I have heard there is a good old Inn at Lancaster, established in a fine old house; an Inn where they give you Bride-cake every day after dinner.'—*The Lazy Tour of Two Idle Apprentices.*

My first impressions of an Inn dated from the Nursery. —*The Holly-Tree.*

Once I passed a fortnight at an Inn in the North of England, where I was haunted by the ghost of a tremendous pie.—*The Holly-Tree.*

... there was such a hurrying up and down stairs of feet, such a glancing of lights, such a whispering of voices, such a smoking and sputtering of wood newly lighted in a damp chimney, such an airing of linen, such a scorching smell of hot warming-pans, such a domestic bustle and to-do, in short as never dragon, griffin, unicorn, or other animal of that species presided over.—The 'Blue Dragon', *Martin Chuzzlewit*.

The Maypole was an old building, with more gable ends than a lazy man would care to count on a sunny day; huge zig-zag chimneys, out of which it seemed as though even smoke could not choose but come in more than naturally fantastic shapes ... its windows were old diamond-pane lattices, its floors were sunken and uneven, its ceilings blackened by the hand of time.—*Barnaby Rudge*.

The Six Jolly Fellowship-Porters, already mentioned as a tavern of a dropsical appearance, had long settled down into a state of hale infirmity. In its whole constitution it had not a straight floor, and hardly a straight line.—*Our Mutual Friend*.

There was an inn in the cathedral town where I went to school, which had pleasanter recollections about it than any of these ... It was the inn where friends used to put up, and where we used to go to see parents, and to have salmon and fowls and be tipped. It had an ecclesiastical sign—the Mitre—and a bar that seemed to be the next best thing to a bishopric, it was so snug.—*The Holly-Tree*.

'We went to the Golden Cross, at Charing Cross, then a mouldy sort of establishment in a close neighbourhood.' —David Copperfield, *David Copperfield*.

'I see myself emerging one evening from some of these [Adelphi] arches, on a little public-house close to the river, with an open space before it, where some coal-heavers were dancing.'—David Copperfield, *David Copperfield*.

'Well, Mr. Raddle,' said Mrs. Bardell, 'I'm sure you ought to feel very much honoured at you and Tommy being the only gentlemen to escort so many ladies all the way to the Spaniards at Hampstead.'—*The Pickwick Papers*.

In the obscure parlour of a low public-house [The Three Cripples], in the filthiest part of Little Saffron Hill; a dark and gloomy den, where a flaring gas-light burnt all day in the winter-time; and where no ray of sun ever shone in the summer . . . —*Oliver Twist*.

The Marquis of Granby in Mrs. Weller's time was quite a model of a road-side public-house of the better class—just large enough to be convenient, and small enough to be snug . . . The bar window displayed a choice collection of geranium plants, and a well-dusted row of spirit phials.—*The Pickwick Papers*.

The Leathern Bottle, a clean and commodious village ale-house . . . at the upper end of the room there was a table, with a white cloth upon it, well covered with a roast fowl, bacon, ale, and et ceteras; and at the table sat Mr. Tupman, looking as unlike a man who had taken his leave of the world, as possible.—*The Pickwick Papers*.

It was one of those unaccountable little rooms which are never seen anywhere but in a tavern, and are supposed to have got into taverns by reason of the facilities afforded to the architect for getting drunk while engaged in their construction.—*Martin Chuzzlewit*.

The Tilted Wagon, as a cool establishment on the top of a hill . . . where everything to drink was drunk out of mugs, and everything else was suggestive of a rhyme to mugs . . . hardly kept its painted promise of providing good entertainment for Man and Beast.—*Edwin Drood*.

This favoured tavern [The Magpie and Stump] . . . was what ordinary people would designate a public-house . . . in the lower windows, which were decorated with curtains of a saffron hue, dangled two or three printed cards, bearing reference to Devonshire cyder and Dantzic spruce . . . the weather-beaten signboard bore the half-obliterated semblance of a magpie intently eyeing a crooked streak of brown paint, which the neighbours had been taught from infancy to consider as the 'stump'.—*The Pickwick Papers*.

GHOSTS AND GOBLINS

'I will die here, where I have walked. And I will walk here, though I am in my grave. I will walk here until the pride of this house is humbled.'—The Ghost of the Round-head Lady Dedlock, *Bleak House*.

'Don't throw that poker at me . . . If you hurled it with ever so sure an aim, it would pass through me, without resistance, and expend its force on the wood behind. I am a spirit.'—The Ghost in Chambers, *The Pickwick Papers*.

'The goblin looked as if he had sat on the same tomb-stone very comfortably, for two or three hundred years. He was sitting perfectly still; his tongue was put out, as if in derision; and he was grinning at Gabriel Grub with such a grin as only a goblin could call up.'—Mr. Wardle, *The Pickwick Papers*.

On the opposite side of the fire, there sat with folded arms a wrinkled hideous figure, with deeply sunk and bloodshot eyes, and an immensely long cadaverous face . . . He wore a kind of tunic . . . clasped and ornamented down the front with coffin handles . . .

'I am the Genius of Despair and Suicide,' said the apparition. 'Now you know me.'—*Nicholas Nickleby*

Marley in his pig-tail, usual waistcoat, tights and boots. . . . The chain he drew was clasped about his middle. It was long, and wound about him like a tail; and it was made . . . of cash-boxes, keys, padlocks, ledgers, deeds, and heavy purses wrought in steel. His body was transparent; so that Scrooge, observing him, and looking through his waistcoat, could see the two buttons on his coat behind.—*A Christmas Carol.*

It [The Ghost of Christmas Past] was a strange figure —like a child; yet not so like a child as like an old man, viewed through some supernatural medium, which gave him the appearance of having receded from the view, and being diminished to a child's proportions. Its hair, which hung about its neck and down its back, was white as if with age; and yet the face had not a wrinkle on it.—*A Christmas Carol.*

He saw the tower, whither his charmed footsteps had brought him, swarming with dwarf phantoms, spirits, elfin creatures of the Bells . . . He saw the air thick with them . . . He saw them riding downward, soaring upward, sailing off afar, perching near at hand, all restless and violently active.—*The Chimes.*

As the gloom and shadow thickened behind him, in that place where it had been gathering so darkly, it took, by slow degrees—or out of it there came, by some unreal, unsubstantial process, not to be traced by any human sense—an awful likeness of himself!—*The Haunted Man.*

The locked door opens, and there comes in a young woman, deadly pale, and with long fair hair, who glides to the fire, and sits down in the chair we have left there, wringing her hands . . . Presently she gets up . . . fixes her eyes on the portrait of the cavalier in green, and says, in a low, terrible voice, 'The stags know it!'—*A Christmas Tree.*

'This gentleman wants to know,' said the landlord, 'if anything's seen at the Poplars.'

''Ooded woman with a howl,' said Ikey, in a state of great freshness.

'Do you mean a cry?'

'I mean a bird, Sir.'

'A hooded woman with an owl. Dear me! Did you ever see her?'

'I seen the howl.'

'Never the woman?'

'Not so plain as the howl, but they always keeps together.'—*The Haunted House.*

'Ah me, ah me! No other ghost has haunted the boy's room, my friends, since I have occupied it, than the ghost of my own childhood, the ghost of my own innocence, the ghost of my own airy belief.'—*The Haunted House.*

'His money could do nothing to save him, and he was hanged. *I* am he, and I was hanged at Lancaster Castle with my face to the wall, a hundred years ago!'—The Ghost of the One Old Man, *The Lazy Tour of Two Idle Apprentices.*

I once saw the apparition of my father . . . He was alive and well, and nothing ever came of it, but I saw him in the daylight, sitting with his back towards me, on a seat that stood beside my bed.—*The Haunted House*.

The figure . . . caught the miniature from the officer, and gave it to me with his own hands, at the same time saying, in a low and hollow tone . . . '*I was younger then, and my face was not then drained of blood.*'—*Dr. Marigold*.

'I wonder what these ghosts of mail coaches carry in their bags,' said the landlord . . .

'The dead letters, of course,' said the Bagman.

'Oh, ah! to be sure,' rejoined the landlord. 'I never thought of that.'—The story of the Bagman's Uncle, *The Pickwick Papers*.

I can no more reconcile the mere banging of doors, ringing of bells, creaking of boards, and such-like insignificances, with the majestic beauty and pervading analogy of all the Divine rules that I am permitted to understand, than I had been able . . . to yoke the spiritual intercourse of my fellow-traveller to the chariot of the rising sun. —*The Haunted House*.

FACES OF CHILDHOOD

The shouts of wonder and delight with which the development of every package was received! The terrible announcement that the baby had been taken in the act of putting a doll's frying-pan into his mouth, and was more than suspected of having swallowed a fictitious turkey glued on a wooden platter! . . . by degrees the children and their emotions got out of the parlour, and by one stair at a time, up to the top of the house.—*A Christmas Carol*.

'Two months and three da-ays! Vaccinated just six weeks ago-o! Took very finely! Considered by the doctor a remarkably beautiful chi-ild! Equal to the general run of children at five months o-old!'—Dot Peerybingle, *The Cricket on the Hearth*.

A face rounded and smoothed by some half-dozen years, but pinched and twisted by the experiences of a life. Bright eyes, but not youthful . . . a baby savage, a young monster, a child who had never been a child.—*The Haunted Man*.

'They are so beautiful!' said Mrs. Kenwigs, sobbing.

'Oh dear,' said all the ladies, 'so they are! it's very natural you should feel proud of that; but don't give way, don't.'

'I can-not help it, and it don't signify,' sobbed Mrs. Kenwigs, 'oh! they're too beautiful to live, much too beautiful!'—*Nicholas Nickleby*.

'Betsy Jane . . . was put upon as that child has been put upon, and changed as that child has changed. I have seen her sit, often and often, think, think, thinking, like him. I have seen her look, often and often, old, old, old, like him.'
—Mrs. Wickam, *Dombey and Son*.

The juggler's wife is less alert than usual with the money-box, for a child's burial has set her thinking that perhaps the baby underneath her shabby shawl may not grow up to be a man, and wear a sky-blue fillet round his head, and salmon-coloured worsted drawers, and tumble in the mud.—*Dombey and Son*.

'Of all the charmin'est infants as ever I heerd tell on, includin' them as was kivered over by the robin-redbreasts arter they'd committed sooicide with blackberries, there never wos any like that 'ere little Tony. He's alvays a-playin' vith a quart pot, that boy is! To see him a settin' down on the doorstep pretending to drink out of it, and fetching a long breath artervards, and smoking a bit of firevood, and sayin', "Now I'm grandfather,"—to see him a-doin' that at two year old is better than any play as wos ever wrote.'—Tony Weller, *Master Humphrey's Clock*.

' . . . and never was a dear child such a brightening thing in a Lodgings or such a playmate to his grandmother as Jemmy to this house and me, and always good and minding what he was told (upon the whole) and soothing for the temper and making everything pleasanter except when he grew old enough to drop his cap down Wozenham's Airy.' —Mrs. Lirriper, *Mrs. Lirriper's Lodgings*.

'Sometimes they would creep under the Tulip-tree, and would sit there with their arms round one another's necks, and their soft cheeks touching, a-reading about the Prince and the Dragon, and the good and bad enchanters, and the king's fair daughter.'—Boots, *The Holly Tree*.

'To five little stone lozenges, each about a foot and a half long, which were . . . sacred to the memory of five little brothers of mine—who gave up trying to get a living exceedingly early in that universal struggle—I am indebted for a belief I religiously entertained that they had all been born on their backs with their hands in their trousers-pockets.'—Pip, *Great Expectations*.

'I slept in a room, a large lonesome room at the top of a house, where there was a trap-door in the ceiling. I have covered my head with the clothes often, not to see it, for it frightened me: a young child with no one near at night.' —Smike, *Nicholas Nickleby*.

No little Gradgrind had ever seen a face in the moon; it was up in the moon before it could speak distinctly. No little Gradgrind had ever learnt the silly jingle, Twinkle, twinkle, little star; how I wonder what you are! No little Gradgrind had ever known wonder on the subject.—*Hard Times*.

'O, here's Charley!' said the boy . . .
It was a thing to look at. The three children close together, and two of them relying solely on the third, and the third so young and yet with an air of age and steadiness that sat so strangely on the childish figure.—*Bleak House*.

'Lord!' says Mr. Bucket, opening his arms, 'here's children too! You may do anything with me, if you only show me children. Give us a kiss, my pets . . . a friend of mine has had nineteen of 'em, ma'am, all by one mother, and she's still as fresh and rosy as the morning.'—*Bleak House*.

The charity children all at once became objects of peculiar and especial interest. The three Miss Browns . . . taught, and exercised, and examined, and re-examined the unfortunate children, until the boys grew pale, and the girls consumptive with study and fatigue.—The Ladies' Societies, *Sketches by Boz*.

'Your future godson is getting on capitally . . . he cries a good deal, and is a very singular colour, which made Jemima and me rather uncomfortable; but as nurse says it's natural, and as of course we know nothing about these things yet, we are quite satisfied with what nurse says.' —The Bloomsbury Christening, *Sketches by Boz*.

They keep a mental almanack with a vast number of Innocents'-days, all in red letters. They recollect the last coronation, because on that day little Tom fell down the kitchen stairs; the anniversary of the Gunpowder Plot, because it was on the fifth of November that Ned asked whether wooden legs were made in heaven and cocked hats grew in gardens.—Sketches of Young Couples.

'She has a beautiful face,' said Trotty.

'Why, yes!... I've thought so many times. I've thought so when my hearth was very cold and cupboard very bare ... But they—they shouldn't try the little face too often, should they, Lilian? That's hardly fair upon a man.'—Will Fern, *The Chimes*.

'I never see any difference in boys. I only know two sorts of boys. Mealy boys, and beef-faced boys.'—Mr. Grimwig, *Oliver Twist*.

It was a very Moloch of a baby, on whose insatiate altar the whole existence of this particular young brother was offered up a daily sacrifice ... Yet Johnny was verily persuaded that it was a faultless baby, without its peer in the realm of England, and was quite content to catch meek glimpses of things in general from behind its skirts, or over its limp flapping bonnet.—*The Haunted Man*.

Master Adolphus was also in the newspaper line of life, being employed ... to vend newspapers at a railway station, where his chubby little person, like a shabbily-disguised Cupid, and his shrill little voice (he was not much more than ten years old) were as well known as the hoarse panting of the locomotives.—*The Haunted Man*.

COUNTRY AND PROVINCIAL

'Kent, sir—everybody knows Kent—apples, cherries, hops and women.'—Jingle, *The Pickwick Papers*.

'Pleasant, pleasant country . . . who could live to gaze from day to day on bricks and slates, who had once felt the influence of a scene like this? Who could continue to exist, where there are no cows but the cows on the chimney-pots; nothing redolent of Pan but pan-tiles; no crop but stone crop?'—Mr. Pickwick, *The Pickwick Papers.*

There are many pleasanter places even in this dreary world, than Marlborough Downs when it blows hard. —*The Pickwick Papers.*

They emerged upon an open park, with an ancient hall, displaying the quaint and picturesque architecture of Elizabeth's time. Long vistas of stately oaks and elm trees appeared on every side . . . 'If this,' said Mr. Pickwick, looking about him, 'If this were the place to which all who are troubled with our friend's complaint came, I fancy their old attachment to this world would very soon return.' —*The Pickwick Papers.*

There is no month in the whole year, in which nature wears a more beautiful appearance than in the month of August.—*The Pickwick Papers.*

'Delightful prospect, Sam,' said Mr. Pickwick.

'Beats the chimley pots, sir,' replied Mr. Weller, touching his hat.—*The Pickwick Papers.*

'As we drew a little nearer [Yarmouth,] and saw the whole adjacent prospect lying a straight line under the sky, I hinted to Peggotty that a mound or so might have improved it; and also that if the land had been a little more separated from the sea, and the town and the tide had not been quite so much mixed up, like toast and water, it would have been nicer.'—David Copperfield, *David Copperfield.*

'I have associated [my mother's picture] ever since, with the sunny street of Canterbury, dozing as it were in the hot light; and with the sight of its old houses and gateways, and the stately, grey Cathedral, with the rooks sailing round the towers.'—David Copperfield, *David Copperfield*.

Sky, sea, beach and village lie as still before us as if they were sitting for the picture. It is dead low-water. A ripple plays among the ripening corn upon the cliff, as if it were faintly trying from recollection to imitate the sea.—Our Watering-Place, *Reprinted Pieces*.

'At last we came into the narrow streets of Deal, and very gloomy they were upon a raw, misty morning. The long, flat beach, with its little irregular houses, wooden and brick, and its litter of capstans, and great boats and sheds . . . wore as dull an appearance as any place I ever saw.'—Esther Summerson, *Bleak House*.

Mr. Winkle . . . walked forth to view the city [of Bristol] which struck him as being a shade more dirty than any place he had ever seen . . . as the pavements of Bristol are not the widest or cleanest upon earth, so its streets are not altogether the straightest or least intricate.—*The Pickwick Papers*.

The red-brown cliffs, richly wooded to their extremest verge, had their softened and beautiful forms reflected in the bluest water, under the clear North Devonshire sky of a November day without a cloud.—*A Message from the Sea*.

Look round and round upon this bare, bleak plain, and see even here, upon a winter's day, how beautiful the shadows are! Alas! it is the nature of their kind to be so. The loveliest things in life, Tom, are but shadows; and they come and go, and change and fade away as rapidly as these!—*Martin Chuzzlewit.*

Mr. Pinch had a shrewd notion that Salisbury was a very desperate sort of place; an exceeding wild and dissipated city . . . he set forth on a stroll about the streets with a vague and not unpleasant idea that they teemed with all kinds of mystery and bedevilment.—*Martin Chuzzlewit.*

'Soon after I was married, I went to Stratford . . . and after we had seen Shakespeare's tomb and birthplace, we went back to the inn there, where we slept that night, and I recollect that all night long I dreamt of nothing but a black gentleman, at full length, in plaster of Paris, with a lay down collar tied with two tassels, leaning against a post and thinking.'—Mrs. Nickleby, *Nicholas Nickleby.*

Snow, wind, ice, and Wolverhampton—all together. No carriage at the station, everything snowed up. So much the better. The Swan will take us under its warm wing, walking or riding. Where is the Swan's nest? In the market-place.—*Miscellaneous Papers.*

The waters are out in Lincolnshire. An arch of the bridge in the park has been sapped and sopped away. The adjacent low-lying ground, for half-a mile in breadth, is a stagnant river, with melancholy trees for islands in it.—*Bleak House.*

[Coketown] was a town of red brick, or of brick that would have been red if the smoke and ashes had allowed it; but as matters stood it was a town of unnatural red and black, like the painted face of a savage. It was a town of machinery and tall chimneys . . . it had a black canal in it, and a river that ran purple with ill-smelling dye.—*Hard Times.*

It is Mr. Goodchild's opinion, that if a visitor on his arrival at Lancaster could be accommodated with a pole which would push the opposite side of the street some yards farther off, it would be better for all parties . . . A place dropped in the midst of a charming landscape, a place with a fine ancient fragment of castle, a place of lovely walks, a place possessing staid old houses richly fitted with old Honduras mahogany.—*The Lazy Tour of Two Idle Apprentices.*

A city of another and a bygone time is Cloisterham, with its hoarse Cathedral-bell, its hoarse rooks hovering about the Cathedral tower, its hoarser and less distinct rooks in the stall far beneath.—*Edwin Drood.*

THE TWO-HEADED EAGLE

'If I know anything of my countrymen, gentlemen, the English heart is stirred by the fluttering of those Stars and Stripes, as it is stirred by no other flag that flies except its own.'—Speech at Delmonico's, 1868.

In all the public establishments of America, the utmost courtesy prevails.—*American Notes.*

Whatever the defects of American universities may be, they disseminate no prejudices; rear no bigots; dig up the buried ashes of no old superstitions; never interpose between the people and their improvement; exclude no man because of his religious opinions; above all . . . recognise a world, and a broad one too, lying beyond the college walls.—*American Notes.*

To an Englishman, accustomed to the paraphernalia of Westminster Hall, an American Court of Law is as odd a sight as, I suppose, an English Court of Law would be to an American.—*American Notes*.

Was there ever such a sunny street as this Broadway. —*American Notes*.

In this district [Fredericksburg], as in all others where slavery sits brooding . . . there is an air of ruin and decay abroad, which is inseparable from the system. —*American Notes*.

Niagara was at once stamped upon my heart, an Image of Beauty; to remain there, changeless and indelible, until its pulses cease to beat, for ever.—*American Notes*.

The American people . . . are, by nature, frank, brave, cordial, hospitable, and affectionate. Cultivation and refinement seem but to enhance their warmth of heart and ardent enthusiasm; and it is the possession of these latter qualities in a most remarkable degree, which renders an educated American one of the most endearing and most generous of friends.'—*American Notes*.

One great blemish in the popular mind of America . . . is Universal Distrust . . . another prominent feature is the love of 'smart' dealing.—*American Notes*.

It would be well, there can be no doubt, for the American people as a whole, if they loved the Real less, and the Ideal somewhat more.—*American Notes*.

'From all that ever I heard about it, I should say America is a very likely sort of place for me to be jolly in!'—Mark Tapley, *Martin Chuzzlewit*.

'We are independent here, sir, . . . we do as we like.' —Jefferson Brick, *Martin Chuzzlewit*.

'I believe no satirist could breathe this air. If another Juvenal or Swift could rise up among us tomorrow, he would be hunted down.'—Mr. Bevan, *Martin Chuzzlewit*.

'Our history commenced at so late a period as to escape the ages of bloodshed and cruelty through which other nations have passed; and so had all the light of their probation, and none of its darkness.'—Mr. Bevan, *Martin Chuzzlewit*.

'Most strangers—and partick'larly Britishers—are much surprised by what they see in the U-nited States,' remarked Mrs. Hominy.

'They have excellent reason to be so, ma'am,' said Martin. 'I never was so much surprised in all my life.' —*Martin Chuzzlewit*.

'Why, I was a-thinking, sir,' returned Mark, 'that if I was a painter and was called upon to paint the American Eagle, how should I do it?'

'Paint it as like an Eagle as you could, I suppose.'

'No,' said Mark. 'That wouldn't do for me, sir. I should want to draw it like a Bat, for its short-sightedness; like a Bantam, for its bragging; like a Magpie, for its honesty; like a Peacock, for its vanity; like a Ostrich, for putting its head in the mud, and thinking nobody sees it—'

'And like a Phoenix, for its power of springing from the ashes of its faults and vices, and soaring up anew into the sky!' said Martin. 'Well, Mark. Let us hope so.'—*Martin Chuzzlewit*.

'LOVELY WOOMAN'

'Tongue; well, that's a wery good thing when it an't a woman's.'—Sam Weller, *The Pickwick Papers*.

'The wictim o' connubiality, as Blue Beard's domestic chaplain said, with a tear of pity, ven he buried him.'—Sam Weller, *The Pickwick Papers.*

'Wen you're a married man, Samivel, you'll understand a good many things as you don't understand now; but vether it's worth while goin' through so much to learn so little as the charity-boy said ven he got to the end of the alphabet, is a matter o' taste.'—Tony Weller, *The Pickwick Papers.*

'We know, Mr. Weller—we, who are men of the world —that a good uniform must work its way with the women, sooner or later.'—The Footman in Blue, *The Pickwick Papers.*

'She's the sort of woman, now' said Mould . . . 'one would almost feel disposed to bury for nothing; and do it neatly, too!'—*Martin Chuzzlewit.*

'Wot's the good o' callin' a young 'ooman a Wenus or a angel, Sammy?'—Tony Weller, *The Pickwick Papers.*

'Be wery careful o' widders all your life, 'specially if they've kept a public house.'—Tony Weller, *The Pickwick Papers.*

'The society of girls is a very delightful thing.' —Traddles, *David Copperfield.*

'English girls not so fine as Spanish—noble creatures— jet hair—black eyes—lovely forms—sweet creatures— beautiful!'—Jingle, *The Pickwick Papers.*

But in some odd nook in Mrs. Todgers' breast, up a great many steps, and in a corner easy to be overlooked, there was a secret door, with 'Woman' written on the spring.—*Martin Chuzzlewit.*

What is prettier than an old lady—except a young lady—when her eyes are bright, when her figure is trim and compact, when her face is cheerful and calm, when her dress is as the dress of a china shepherdess?—*Edwin Drood.*

Nature often enshrines gallant and noble hearts in weak bosoms—oftenest, God bless her, in female breasts.—*The Old Curiosity Shop.*

'I shall wear this emblem of woman's perfidy, in remembrance of her with whom I shall never again thread the windings of the mazy; whom I shall never more pledge in the rosy.'—Dick Swiveller, *The Old Curiosity Shop.*

'Accidents will occur in the best-regulated families; and in families not regulated by that pervading influence which sanctifies while it enhances the —a—I would say, in short, by the influence of Woman, in the lofty character of Wife, they may be expected with confidence, and must be borne with philosophy.'—Mr. Micawber, *David Copperfield.*

'Wooman, lovely Wooman, what a sex you are!'—Mr. Turveydrop, *Bleak House.*

It has been often enough remarked that women have a curious power of divining the characters of men; which would seem to be innate and instinctive.—*Edwin Drood.*

'In respect of the great necessity there is, my darling, for more employments being within the reach of Woman than our civilization has as yet assigned to her, don't fly at the unfortunate men, even those men who are at first sight in your way, as if they were the natural oppressors of your sex.'—*The Haunted House.*

THE FESTIVE BOARD

It *was* a turkey! He never could have stood upon his legs, that bird. He would have snapped 'em short off in a minute, like sticks of sealing-wax.—*A Christmas Carol.*

A highly geological home-made cake.—*Martin Chuzzlewit.*

'Let us be merry.' Here he took a captain's biscuit.—Mr. Pecksniff, *Martin Chuzzlewit.*

'Mrs. Harris,' I says, 'leave the bottle on the chimley-piece, and don't ask me to take none, but let me put my lips to it when I am so dispoged.'—Mrs. Gamp, *Martin Chuzzlewit.*

'Therefore I *do* require it, which I makes confession, to be brought reg'lar and draw'd mild.'—Mrs. Gamp, *Martin Chuzzlewit.*

'Bring in the bottled lightning, a clean tumbler, and a corkscrew.'—The Gentleman in Small-clothes, *Nicholas Nickleby.*

'Fan the sinking flame of hilarity with the wing of friendship and pass the rosy wine.'—Dick Swiveller, *The Old Curiosity Shop.*

'Did you ever taste beer?' 'I had a sip of it once,' said the small servant. 'Here's a state of things!' cried Mr. Swiveller . . . 'She *never* tasted it—it can't be tasted in a sip!'—*The Old Curiosity Shop.*

'I'll eat my head.'—Mr. Grimwig, *Oliver Twist.*

'Meaty jelly, too, especially when a little salt, which is the case when there's ham, is mellering to the organ.' —Silas Wegg, *Our Mutual Friend*.

'Five children—mother—tall lady, eating sandwiches—forgot the arch—crash—knock—children look round—mother's head off—sandwich in her hand—no mouth to put it in—head of a family off—shocking, shocking!'—Jingle, *The Pickwick Papers*.

'Half-a-crown in the bill, if you look at the waiter. Charge you more if you dine at a friend's than they would if you dined in the coffee-room.'—Jingle, *The Pickwick Papers*.

'It wasn't the wine,' murmured Mr. Snodgrass, in a broken voice. 'It was the salmon.'—*The Pickwick Papers*.

'A double glass o' the inwariable.'—Tony Weller, *The Pickwick Papers*.

'It's my opinion, sir, that this meeting is drunk, sir!' —Mr. Stiggins, *The Pickwick Papers*.

'Chops and tomato sauce. Yours, Pickwick.'—Mr. Pickwick, *The Pickwick Papers*.

'Which is your partickler wanity? Vich wanity do you like the flavour on best, sir?'—Sam Weller, *The Pickwick Papers*.

'A friendly swarry, consisting of a boiled leg of mutton with the usual trimmings.'—*The Pickwick Papers*.

'Not presume to dictate, but broiled fowl and mush-rooms—capital thing!'—Jingle, *The Pickwick Papers*.

'May we never want a friend in need, nor a bottle to give him!'—Captain Cuttle, *Dombey and Son*.

'What is the odds so long as the fire of soul is kindled at the taper of conwiviality, and the wing of friendship never moults a feather.'—Dick Swiveller, *The Old Curiosity Shop*.

'Do you ever drink anythin'?' asked Sam.
'I likes eating better,' replied the boy.—*The Pickwick Papers*.

'Soles—ah! capital fish—all come from London—stage-coach proprietors get up political dinners—carriage of soles—dozens of baskets—cunning fellows.'—Jingle, *The Pickwick Papers*.

Indistinct visions of rook-pie floated through [The Fat Boy's] imagination. He laughed as he retired with the bird—it was a plump one.—*The Pickwick Papers*.

What a dinner! specimens of all the fishes that swim in the sea surely had swum their way to it . . . and the dishes being seasoned with Bliss . . . were of perfect flavour, and the golden drinks had been bottled in the golden age and hoarding up their sparkles ever since.—*Our Mutual Friend*.

At long intervals were uncomfortable refreshment-rooms . . . where sensitive stomachs were fed, with a contemptuous sharpness occasioning indigestion.—*The Lazy Tour of Two Idle Apprentices*.

Even the street was made a fairy street, by being half hidden in an atmosphere of steak, and strong, stout, stand-up English beer.—*Martin Chuzzlewit*.

'I like this plan of sending 'em with the peel on; there's a charm in drawing a potato from its native element (if I may so express it) to which the rich and powerful are strangers.'—Dick Swiveller, *The Old Curiosity Shop*.

'Think of this wine, for instance . . . which has been to the East Indies and back, I'm not able to say how often, and has been once round the world. Think of the pitch-dark nights, the roaring winds, and rolling seas.'—Sol Gills, *Dombey and Son*.

'I have got a cold fillet of veal here, Sir.' replied Mr. Chick, rubbing his numbed hands together. 'What have *you* got there, sir?'

'This,' returned Mr. Dombey, 'is some cold preparation of calf's head, I think. I see cold fowls—ham—patties—salad—lobster.'—*Dombey and Son*.

'A nice small kidney-pudding, now, Cap'en Cuttle,' said his landlady, 'or a sheep's heart. Don't mind my trouble.'

'No thank'ee, Ma'am,' returned the Captain.

'Have a roast fowl . . . with a bit of weal stuffing and some egg sauce. Come, Cap'en Cuttle! give yourself a little treat.'—*Dombey and Son*.

'We have but a shoulder of mutton with onion sauce,' said Mrs. Crummles, in the same charnel-house voice; 'but such as our dinner is, we beg you to partake of it.' —*Nicholas Nickleby*.

Surely she was the best sauce for chops ever invented. The potatoes seemed to take a pleasure in sending up their grateful steam before her; the froth upon the pint of porter pouted to attract her notice.—*Martin Chuzzlewit*.

'*You* make a beef-steak pudding, indeed!' said Tom, giving her a gentle push. 'Why, you haven't boldness enough for a dumpling!'

'You *will* call it a pudding, Tom. Mind! I told you not!'
'I may as well call it that, till it proves to be something else.'—Tom and Ruth Pinch, *Martin Chuzzlewit*.

I am hungry when I arrive at the [railway] Refreshment station . . . I turn my disconsolate eyes on the refreshments that are to restore me. I find that I must either scal my throat by insanely ladling into it . . . brown hot water stiffened with flour . . . or I must extort from an iron-bound quarry, with a fork, as if I were farming an inhospitable soil, some glutinous lumps of gristle and grease, called pork-pie.—*The Uncommercial Traveller*.

'Wery good thing is weal pie, when you know the lady as made it, and is quite sure it ain't kittens.'—Sam Weller, *The Pickwick Papers*.

MERRY CHRISTMAS

That man must be a misanthrope indeed, in whose breast something like a jovial feeling is not roused—in whose mind some pleasant associations are not awakened —by the recurrence of Christmas.—A Christmas Dinner, *Sketches by Boz*.

Reflect upon your present blessings . . . not your past misfortunes . . . fill your glass again, with a merry face and contented heart. Our life on it, but your Christmas shall be merry, and your New Year a happy one!—A Christmas Dinner, *Sketches by Boz*.

There seems a magic in the very name of Christmas.— A Christmas Dinner, *Sketches by Boz*.

'I do not fit smoothly into the social circle, and consequently I have no other engagement at Christmas-time than to partake, on the twenty-fifth, of a boiled turkey and celery sauce.'—Mr. Grewgious, *Edwin Drood*.

Christmas Eve in Cloisterham . . . Seasonable tokens are about. Red berries shine here and there in the lattices of Minor Canon Corner . . . Lavish profusion is in the shops; particularly in the articles of currants, raisins, spices, candied peel, and moist sugar.—*Edwin Drood*.

'Our invariable custom . . . everybody sits down with us on Christmas Eve, as you see them now—servants and all; and here we wait, until the clock strikes twelve, to usher Christmas in, and beguile the time with forfeits and old stories.'—Mr. Wardle, *The Pickwick Papers*.

> 'But my song I troll out, for CHRISTMAS stout,
> The hearty, the true, and the bold;
> A bumper I drain, and with might and main
> Give three cheers for this Christmas old!
> We'll usher him in with a merry din
> That shall gladden his joyous heart,
> And we'll keep him up, while there's bite or sup,
> And in fellowship good, we'll part.
>
> In his fine honest pride, he scorns to hide
> One jot of his hard-weather scars;
> They're no disgrace, for there's much the same trace
> On the cheeks of our bravest tars.
> Then again I'll sing, till the roof doth ring,
> And it echoes from wall to wall—
> To the stout old wight, fair welcome tonight,
> As the King of the Seasons all!'
>   —Mr. Wardle, *The Pickwick Papers*.

Comes swift to comfort me, the Pantomime—stupendous Phenomenon! when clowns are shot from loaded mortars into the great chandelier, bright constellation that it is; when Harlequins, covered all over with scales of pure gold, twist and sparkle, like amazing fish . . . —A Christmas Tree, *Christmas Stories*.

And I *do* come home at Christmas. We all do, or we all should . . . for a short holiday—the longer, the better—from the great boarding-school . . . to take, and give a rest. —A Christmas Tree, *Christmas Stories*.

Encircled by the social thoughts of Christmas-time, still let the benignant figure of my childhood stand unchanged! In every cheerful image and suggestion that the season brings, may the bright star that rested above the poor roof, be the star of all the Christian world!—A Christmas Tree, *Christmas Stories*.

Nearer and closer to our hearts be the Christmas spirit, which is the spirit of active usefulness, perseverance, cheerful discharge of duty, kindness and forbearance!—What Christmas is as we grow older, *Christmas Stories*.

On Christmas Day, we will shut out from our fireside, Nothing.—What Christmas is as we grow older, *Christmas Stories*.

I began at the Holly-Tree . . . to associate the Christmas-time of year with human interest, and with some inquiry into, and some care for, the lives of those by whom I find myself surrounded.—The Holly-Tree, *Christmas Stories*.

'Merry Christmas! out upon Merry Christmas! What's Christmas time to you but a time for paying bills without money; a time for finding yourself a year older, but not an hour richer; a time for balancing your books, and having every item in 'em through a round dozen of months presented dead against you? If I could work my will . . . every idiot who goes about with "Merry Christmas" on his lips should be boiled with his own pudding, and buried with a stake of holly through his heart.'—Scrooge, *A Christmas Carol*.

'I don't make merry myself at Christmas and I can't afford to make idle people merry.'—Scrooge, *A Christmas Carol*.

Holly, mistletoe, red berries, ivy, turkeys, geese, game, poultry, brawn, meat, pigs, sausages, oysters, pies, puddings, fruit and punch, all vanished instantly. So did the room, the fire, the ruddy glow, the hour of night; and they stood in the city streets on Christmas morning, where (for the weather was severe) the people made a rough but brisk and not unpleasant kind of music, in scraping the snow from the pavement in front of their dwellings. —*A Christmas Carol*.

They said it was a shame to quarrel upon Christmas Day. And so it was! God love it, so it was!—*A Christmas Carol*.

It is good to be children sometimes, and never better than at Christmas, when its mighty Founder was a child Himself.—*A Christmas Carol*.

'I will honour Christmas in my heart, and try to keep it all the year. I will live in the Past, the Present, and the Future.'—Scrooge, *A Christmas Carol*.

'Another Christmas come, another year gone! More figures in the lengthening sum of recollection that we work and work at to our torment, till Death idly jumbles all together, and rubs all out.'—Redlaw, *The Haunted Man*.

'It seems to me as if the birth-time of Our Lord was the birth-time of all I have ever had affection for, or mourned for, or delighted in.'—Philip Swidger, *The Haunted Man*.

HOUSEHOLD WORDS

'God bless us, every one!'—Tiny Tim, *A Christmas Carol*.

'I am a lone creetur' . . . and everythink goes contrairy with me.'—Mrs. Gummidge, *David Copperfield*.

'Barkis is willin'.'—*David Copperfield*.

'I never will desert Mr. Micawber.'—Mrs. Micawber, *David Copperfield*.

'We are so very 'umble.'—Uriah Heep, *David Copperfield*.

' "In case anything turned up" . . . was his favourite expression'—Mr. Micawber, *David Copperfield*.

'I only ask for information.'—Rosa Dartle, *David Copperfield*.

'It's of no consequence, thank'ee.'—Mr. Toots, *Dombey and Son*.

'There's milestones on the Dover Road!'—Mr. F.'s Aunt, *Little Dorrit*.

'Bother Mrs. Harris!' said Betsey Prig . . . 'I don't believe there's no sich a person!'—*Martin Chuzzlewit*.

'C-l-e-a-n, clean, verb active, to make bright, to scour. W-i-n, win, d-e-r, winder, a casement. When the boy knows this out of the book, he goes and does it.'—Mr. Squeers, *Nicholas Nickleby*.

'A demd, damp, moist, unpleasant body.'—Mr. Mantalini, *Nicholas Nickleby*.

'All is gas and gaiters.'—The Gentleman in Smallclothes, *Nicholas Nickleby*.

'Codlin's the friend, not Short.'—Codlin, *The Old Curiosity Shop*.

'Please, sir, I want some more!'—Oliver, *Oliver Twist*.

'If the law supposes that,' said Mr. Bumble . . . 'the law is a ass.'—*Oliver Twist*.

'Put it down a we, my Lord, put it down a we.'—Tony Weller, *The Pickwick Papers*.

'Oh Sammy, Sammy, vy worn't there a alleybi!'—Tony Weller, *The Pickwick Papers*.

'It is a far, far better thing that I do, than I have ever done; it is a far, far better rest that I go to, than I have ever known.'—Sydney Carton, *A Tale of Two Cities*.

'I wants to make your flesh creep.'—The Fat Boy, *The Pickwick Papers*.

'He has gone to the demnition bow-wows.'—Mr. Mantalini, *Nicholas Nickleby*.

'When found, make a note of.'—Captain Cuttle, *Dombey and Son*.

'Here's richness!'—Mr. Squeers, *Nicholas Nickleby*.

'She's a swellin' wisibly before my wery eyes.'—Tony Weller, *The Pickwick Papers*.

'Do you recollect the date,' said Mr. Dick, ' . . . when King Charles the First had his head cut off?'—*David Copperfield*.

Mr. Weller's knowledge of London was extensive and peculiar.—*The Pickwick Papers*.

CHARLES DICKENS

THE LIFE OF DICKENS

The man who was to become the Genius, or presiding
deity, of Low Life was born fairly and squarely into
the middle of society. His paternal grandfather, William
Dickens, had started life as a footman, and had later
become a steward; and his grandmother had risen from
housemaid to housekeeper. They had given their son,
John Dickens, an excellent start in life as a clerk in the
Navy Pay Office. There he met young Thomas Barrow,
whose sister, Elizabeth, he was to marry in 1809. The
Barrows could claim relationship with Sir John Barrow,
second secretary of the Admiralty from 1804 to 1845.
Charles Barrow, John Dickens's father-in-law, held a
substantial appointment under the Navy Board, but threw
it away through something suspiciously like embezzle-
ment.

There was, in fact, a solid middle-class background to
the baby Charles Dickens, born at 387 Commercial Road,
Landport, in the Portsea district of Portsmouth, on
February 7th, 1812. Aquarius was his birth-sign, and if
there be any truth in astrology, here was a true Aquarian
child, born to be a lover of his fellow-men, a reformer, a
good friend but a difficult man to have in the family.
None of these developments, however, seemed very
likely in the early years of Charles's life, which were
heavily overshadowed by such insecurity as might have
ruined the character of a lesser man.

From the evidence we have, it seems that this originated
in the weakness of John Dickens, his father. John, who was
later to be transmogrified into Wilkins Micawber, was a
cheerful, feckless man, beloved by his family but hope-
lessly inept at providing for them. In 1824 he was arrested
for debt, and ten years later was again arrested and

imprisoned in the debtors' prison, the Marshalsea, in the Borough district near London Bridge; that place of such horror to the young Charles, who wrote it out of his system in *Little Dorrit*—with his father again mirrored in William Dorrit, the prison's patriarch.

We know little of Mrs. Dickens in these years. She had five children to rear, and her time must have been fully taken up by them and in organizing the family removals from Portsea to London (1814), from London to Chatham (1817), and back to London in the winter of 1822. But Charles did not accompany the family on this last move; he was left at day school in Chatham, a place which he made his own and which helped substantially to make him.

At Chatham, he and his elder sister Fanny, to whom he was deeply attached, had a young nursemaid, Mary Weller, who was a great story-teller and something of an expert on ghosts, goblins, and horrifying legends. Between her tales, and his own tremendous capacity for reading, Charles's mind was enriched and his imagination fed until it thrived wondrously. In *David Copperfield*, the book which was to contain more of the facts of his own life than any of his other works, he tells of the attic room which contained his precious books: 'From that blessed little room, Roderick Random, Peregrine Pickle, Humphrey Clinker, Tom Jones, The Vicar of Wakefield, Don Quixote, Gil Blas, and Robinson Crusoe came out, a glorious host to keep me company.'

William Giles, his schoolmaster, appreciated the possibilities of his bright pupil, and gave him unreservedly the education which his mind drank in so eagerly. But it was not to last. In the spring of 1823, when he was eleven, Charles was sent for to join his family in London. They were living in Bayham Street, Camden Town; a district now remarkable for its drab ugliness, but in those days unspoilt by the advent of the railway and the subsequent avalanche of bricks and mortar which came with it. The surroundings were not so bad: but the home conditions Charles found at Bayham Street were very bad indeed. He, the bright scholar and romantic dreamer of Chatham, was now the family drudge and errand-goer. There was no talk of further schooling for him. Many years later he told Forster, his friend and biographer:

'As I thought in the little back-garret at Bayham-street, of all I had lost in losing Chatham, what would I have given, if I had had anything to give, to have been sent back to any other school, to have been taught something anywhere!'

His mother tried to retrieve the family fortunes by starting a school herself. A brass plate went up at 4 Gower Street, where the Dickens family was now living; notices went out (distributed by Charles and his brothers and sisters), but nobody came to 'Mrs. Dickens's Establishment for young Ladies'. Charles's cherished books were sold to bring in a little money. The boy's one pleasure now was the discovery of London. 'To be taken out for a walk into the real town, especially if it were anywhere about Covent-Garden or the Strand, perfectly entranced him with pleasure.' Nineteenth-century London, the sordid, bustling, foggy, frowsty city which was to become known as 'Dickens's London', seethed and roared about the small, wistful, eleven-year-old figure in its thin boots and tight, outgrown clothes. His wanderings were soon to be limited.

When finances were at their lowest at home, an offer arrived of work for Charles. A cousin, James Lamert, volunteered to take him on at Warren's Blacking Factory, at Hungerford Stairs, Charing Cross, at a wage of six shillings a week. It happened on his twelfth birthday, which must have accentuated the bitterness of the blow. In those days children worked as a matter of course, and the Dickens parents—never remarkable for their sensitivity—seem to have felt no compunction about sending the delicate, clever child to that crazy, tumble-down old house on the river, swarming with rats and noisome with dirt and decay. In adult life Dickens wrote much about that blacking factory. Blacking was to haunt his mind as long as he lived, like one of those warning phantoms that abound in his books. He wrote of it with sick bitterness. From the man who was a great author, a success, head of a family, friend of thousands, there was, not very far away, the spectre of that small boy whom we glimpse in *The Haunted House*: 'Master B.'—who is, of course, Master Boz—'the ghost of my own innocence, the ghost of my own airy belief'. There he sat for ever, in Dickens's mind, the poor little ghost, labelling pots of paste-blacking, hopeless and degraded in his own eyes. It is impossible to over-estimate the effect of this episode on Dickens's character, on his attitude to worldly success, his relationships—and his writings.

This dreadful period of his life had only just begun when another blow fell: his father was arrested for debt and sent to the Marshalsea. Mrs. Dickens and the younger children followed him, and Charles was found a lodging which was a certain improvement on the first one he had had (at which he found the grim original of Mrs. Pipchin). Then, suddenly, came a legacy which cleared John Dickens's debts. The Dickenses moved out of the Marshalsea, and a family quarrel had the happy result of taking Charles away from the blacking factory. His mother tried to patch up the quarrel, and organized a request from Warren's that Charles should be sent back there. He never forgot it, nor forgave her.

At last his education was resumed. He was sent to Wellington House Academy, at the corner of Granby Street and Hampstead Road. The house still stood until late in 1964, an unattractive shell only fit for demolition; but in its time it brought Dickens the education he craved and a measure of normality. Its headmaster, Mr. Jones, seems to have been the prototype of the fiery Creakle, but apart from his fondness for the application of the ruler to small boys' hands, the school has nothing in common with that nightmare one attended by David Copperfield. There were pet white mice, a secret language, and a fair amount of fun and mischief, in which Charles was active. He had recovered his spirits, and apparently was growing out of his early delicacy. Here for the first time we hear of his writing small tales, and circulating them among his fellow-students; and of his being a leader in school dramatics—a foreshadowing of his later love for acting.

He stayed at Wellington House Academy for two years. In spring, 1827, he left to become office-boy to Charles Molloy, a solicitor of Symonds Inn. After a few weeks he moved on to the firm of Ellis and Blackmore, of Gray's Inn, and here he stayed for a year, occupying his spare time in learning shorthand, with the intention of following in the footsteps of his father, now a Parliamentary reporter. 'Whatever I have tried to do in life,' he later said, 'I have tried with all my heart to do well.' His tremendous application and enthusiasm soon made him a skilled short-hand writer, but Parliamentary reporting was not yet for him. He had two years to pass as reporter for a legal office, working away happily enough and acquiring that know-ledge of the law and its delays, humours and horrors which permeates his books.

At this 'highly unsubstantial, happy, foolish time', as Forster calls it, a new element filled his life. He was in love. Maria Beadnell was the daughter of a bank manager, pretty, accomplished and flirtatious. Charles was by now good value as a social entertainer. Always to be the life and soul of any party, he could sing comic songs, dance the hornpipe, tell amusing but respectable stories, and write light verse for his own recitation; just the accomplishments to appeal to a frivolous young lady. Maria's family had no serious thought of the penniless reporter as a husband for their daughter, but it seems that some sort of secret engagement was made between the two young people. It lasted for two years, and Charles worked hard to better himself for Maria's sake. Then Maria was sent off to Paris to finish her education, and this was the end of the romance. Dickens wrote to her that their recent meetings had been little more than displays of heartless indifference on her part. He returned her presents, and determined to make his life without her. But his passion for Maria had gone deep into his soul; it was no light boyhood thing, to be briefly regretted and quickly forgotten. On his violently impressionable nature it made a mark only comparable with that left by the blacking factory. Love, and love slighted, and frivolous, pretty girlhood, were to be for ever Maria Beadnell. Only one other woman, also to be lost to him, ever made such an impression again. Maria, translated into fictional terms, became the adorable, useless Dora, Copperfield's child-bride, and later—when Dickens had met her again, in the too-solid middle-aged flesh—the silly, blowsy Flora Finching of *Little Dorrit*.

He was broken-hearted when the affair with Maria ended. The blow was partially softened by his achievement of an ambition—to become a Parliamentary reporter. He joined the *True Sun*, on which journal he met John Forster, who was to become his lifelong friend, and on the first day of its publication in March, 1832, he found himself in the House of Commons, taking down the last speeches made during the Committee stage of the Reform Bill. For the *True Sun*, a journal called the *Mirror of Parliament*, and for the *Morning Chronicle*, he reported for four hard years, sparing no effort and meeting with the countless obstacles which in those days beset young reporters: ' . . . writing,' he says, 'on the palm of my hand, by the light of a dark lantern, in a post-chaise and four, galloping through a wild country, and through the dead of the night.'

It was tremendously important experience for that lively, developing mind. He saw politicians in action; he learnt of the conditions which prevailed, and which needed reform. Since his hard boyhood he had been aware of poverty, slum dwellings, the lack of education for young people of the humbler kind, or the provision of an education merely perfunctory and administered with casual cruelty. He had seen the debtor's prison and the pawnshop, had been himself involved in their miseries and humiliations. Now he began to apply the lessons he had learnt to social issues. He travelled far and wide, and saw England of the early 1830's with all her imperfections thick upon her. Injustice, oppression, all the horrors of the 'work'us' revealed in the Poor Law Bill which he reported, sank into his brain and bred ideas there.

Success came to him easily as a reporter—'A more talented reporter never sat in the Gallery,' said James Grant of the *Morning Advertiser*. But the writing of shorthand was not enough for Charles Dickens: he turned his mind to authorship. Since childhood he had been interested in the miscellany form of literature—collected sketches and essays on different subjects. Now, in 1836, he began to collect into two volumes some sketches he had contributed to *The Monthly Magazine* and other periodicals, which he called *Sketches by Boz*—Boz being the family nickname of his little brother which he now adopted as a pseudonym. Dickens, with tears in his eyes as he read his first published work, cared nothing for money, though he was earning little enough at the time and his ever-demanding family was drawing on his small resources. He continued to write, and the *Sketches* attracted attention. They were a little naïve, but vigorous and professional. His identity became known, and he was approached by Mr. Hall, a partner of the newly formed publishing firm of

Chapman and Hall, to provide copy to accompany sporting sketches by the artist Robert Seymour. Sport was not a favourite subject of the young Mr. Dickens—but a chance was a chance, and he took it. *The Times* of March 26th, 1836, gave notice that on the 31st would be published the first shilling number of *The Posthumous Papers of the Pickwick Club.*

The theme of sport was soon forgotten as Pickwick found his feet. What was to have been a rather pedestrian sequence of contemporary sporting humours became the most ebullient, irresistible comic book ever to have been written by an Englishman. It gave to literature at least two characters of deathless fame—Pickwick and Sam Weller—and a bottomless well of quotation. For those who learn to love it early, it is the funny book of all time: the voice of humorous reason speaking to the young and solemn nineteenth century. Whatever Dickens was to write later, there are things in *Pickwick* that he never paralleled.

Two days after the publication of *The Pickwick Papers*, Dickens was married. He had wooed and won Catherine Hogarth, daughter of a colleague on the *Morning Chronicle*; an amiable young woman with a sensuously pretty face and a lazy manner. She was the eldest of three sisters. Georgina, the youngest, was still a child, but Mary was sixteen and very charming 'So perfect a creature never breathed. She had not a fault,' Dickens said of her. When, in 1837, the young couple and their newly born son moved into a house in Doughty Street, Bloomsbury, Mary went with them to be company for Kate and help her with the baby. Mary was a robust, merry girl, and it was a happy little family that inhabited the house which is now the headquarters of the Dickens Fellowship. But the happiness was short-lived. One night after returning from the theatre Mary was taken ill and died the next day. With no previous sign or warning, her light was extinguished all in a moment. Like the experiences at the blacking factory, like Maria Beadnell's rejection, Mary's death burnt itself into his mind and branded it for ever. He wore her ring on his finger until his own death, and for years was haunted by a recurrent dream or vision of her. This sorrow is suffered, over and over again, in his books —in the death of Little Nell, in the nearly fatal illness of Rose Maylie, in the death of Dora. Had she been his wife or his betrothed, his mourning could not have been greater; yet at the time of her death he was a newly married man, and there was no thought of illicit love in his mind. It is one of the great puzzles—all concerned with women—which Dickens's life presents to biographers. With the relationship of marriage he deals conventionally, but without much warmth or conviction. All his passion and pathos and real feeling are spent on the prohibited degrees of kindred—Rumty Wilfer and his daughter Bella, Scrooge and his sister, Paul and Florence Dombey; and many more.

Before *Pickwick* was ended he began his first serious novel, *Oliver Twist*, that cry of anger against the workhouse system, the cruelties and injustices and corruption that beset helpless children. Oliver himself is a colourless infant, too good to live; but his story effectively criticized the Poor Law which Dickens resented so much. The writing of it had an enormous effect upon him. As Forster says, 'The book itself, in teaching him what his power was, had made him more conscious of what would be expected from its use; and this never afterwards quitted him.' With the humour of *Pickwick* was a leavening of the grimmer side of life—the debtors' prison, from which even the jovial Pickwick emerges not quite the same man, the death of the Chancery prisoner, the story of the drunkard's end, the pathetic decline of Jingle—all these gave his readers a sense that there were wrongs to be righted. It was this marvellous balance between laughter and tears

which was to make Dickens the greatest of literary re-
formers.

By this time in his life his personality was coming into
full flower; and a spectacular bloom it was. Not for him the
authorship which puts all its strength, wit and passion into
print, and leaves the author himself limp and socially
disappointing. His appearance attracted many artists, and
his quality shines out brilliantly from the full-length
portrait Maclise made of him in 1839. Dickens sits at a
table, one hand resting upon a manuscript. His clothes,
though not as gorgeous as those he sometimes affected,
have an air of richness; he has obviously enjoyed choosing
them and putting them on. His face is turned towards the
window, as if seeking inspiration from the light—a face of
vivid sensitivity, almost feminine in its delicacy; the large
eyes shining with intelligence, the charming sensual mouth
not yet hidden by whiskers, the long hair falling casually
over one temple. One who knew him at this time said of
him: 'He seemed all on fire with curiosity, and alive as I
never saw mortal before.' Another remarked that 'the
mere thrill of his wonderful voice had a magic of persuasion
in it'. Yet no verbal description can convey the man as
vividly as Maclise's brush has done. A drawing of 1844,
also by Maclise, is equally illuminating. He sits reading
The Chimes to a circle of friends, his head encircled by an
aureole.

A new book had begun as *Oliver Twist* ended. It was
Nicholas Nickleby, a romantic story with an impulsive,
chivalrous young hero and a host of immortal characters.
'Here's richness!' as one of them observes. The action
ranges from London offices, through the salon of a fashionable bonnet-maker, to a company of actors in Portsmouth—
and up to Yorkshire. For this agreeable novel, which owes
so much to *Tom Jones* and *Humphrey Clinker*, had an
axe to grind in the North. Dickens had been haunted since
childhood by a story he had heard about the notorious

'Yorkshire Schools': cheap boarding-schools run entirely for profit, where unwanted boys, usually illegitimate, were farmed out and kept under miserable conditions. These Dickens inspected personally, and epitomized them in their full horror as 'Dotheboys Hall', where Nicholas became an usher until the brutalities he witnessed drove him to attack the schoolmaster, Squeers, and shake the dust of the place from his feet. Dickens always insisted that Dotheboys Hall was but 'a faint and feeble picture of an existing reality'. The consternation aroused by it in the public mind led to the closing of the Yorkshire Schools. Dickens had dealt another of his blows with the pen.

The Dickens family moved in 1839 from Doughty Street to 1, Devonshire Terrace, Marylebone; a house now regrettably pulled down and replaced by a hideous office block bearing an apologetic Dickensian bas-relief. One of the present authors lived in the house for a time, and rejoiced in the reminders it provided at every turn of the works written there. Up the elegant staircase Florence Dombey had toiled, little Paul in her arms. Through the french window, down two steps, was the neglected garden in which Grip the raven had played with the Dickens children, while upstairs their father wrote him into *Barnaby Rudge*. In the kitchen below stairs the cricket had sung on the hearth, Master Humphrey's clock had ticked in the elegant hall.

Master Humphrey's Clock was a series of stories linked by the central figure of a crippled old man. Some of these were short tales or episodes, re-introducing Mr. Pickwick and the Wellers; but interspersed with them were two novels in serial form, *The Old Curiosity Shop* and *Barnaby Rudge*. The first was a panoramic novel presenting the world with such characters as Dick Swiveller and his Marchioness, Codlin and Short, the Punch and Judy men, Mrs. Jarley the waxworks queen, and most vital of all, Quilp, a horrible dwarf of hypnotic charm. But the world ignored these in favour of the book's heroine, Little Nell, the child whose weary travels with her useless old grandfather end in her death. She is a sentimentalized, unreal figure by modern standards, but Dickens put into her much of the grief which had been stored up since Mary Hogarth died. 'Dear Mary died yesterday, when I think of this sad story', he wrote after the killing-off of Nell. Dickens's public, on both sides of the Atlantic, wept with him, and his fame was cemented by their tears.

Barnaby Rudge was an historical novel of the days of the Gordon riots, the action moving between Essex and London. It proved less popular; yet Dolly Varden, the blacksmith's lovely daughter, became an instant favourite, and gave her name to a coquettish bonnet: and Barnaby, the gentle idiot, and his raven friend Grip have a real pathos in contrast to the saccharine quality of Little Nell.

1841 saw Dickens in America, enjoying a working holiday at his publishers' expense. Kate was with him, resigned to the upheaval but not enjoying herself; the four children remained at home with the family of the actor Macready. Dickens was lionized, wined, dined, lauded, made the subject of odes by intense American poetesses. The classlessness of America appealed to his democratic sense, but he found much to dislike; and in *American Notes* (1843) and *Martin Chuzzlewit*, his next novel, he satirized these things freely. He had somewhat lessened his welcome in America by strenuous propaganda for international copyright—the situation then being that the Americans were at liberty to reprint any English book without any communication with or payment to the author. This form of piracy infuriated Dickens, and he constituted himself the champion of his fellow-authors, though without result in his own lifetime.

Martin Chuzzlewit displeased America, but the British public took to its heart the drunken midwife Mrs. Gamp, the cheerful Mark Tapley, and the arch-hypocrite Peck-sniff. The book contains Dickens's nastiest villain, Jonas Chuzzlewit, and his nearest approach so far to a real woman in Mercy Chuzzlewit, the giggling girl who marries to spite her sister and is shocked by marital misery into womanhood. Dickens was rapidly maturing as a writer by this date (1843). His humour was rich and fertile, his satire sharp, his social criticism biting; but in the portrayal of the characters about whom he himself felt most deeply he could not rise above the sentimental. *Dombey and Son*, published in 1846, showed to full advantage his powers of comic and dramatic invention; however, to him—and his public—the strongest interest lay in little Paul Dombey, the angel-child who was to die at six years old, seeing a vision of his dead mother coming towards him in the path of the sunbeams. In *A Christmas Carol* the crippled form of Tiny Tim takes the centre of the stage. In the *Carol* Dickens was able to return to his special pleading for the poor, and to identify himself with the spirit of Christmas. If he did not quite invent the English Christmas, as has sometimes been said, he made of it something it had never been before. Christianity to Dickens was something instinctive, although he found it very difficult to settle down with any particular church. Roman Catholic, Anglican and Noncomformist are satirized in his works, and if he finally settled for the Anglican form of worship, it was very much *faute de mieux*. The requirements of Victorian respectability demanded his adherence to one or another, just as he was expected, in his role of pater-familias, to sire ten children, with at least nine of whom he could well have dispensed, though he loved them when they arrived, and took his fatherhood seriously.

In 1848 his eighth child and sixth son was born, and his newest work—*David Copperfield*. For the first time the story was told in the first person, and for a very good reason: much of it was Dickens's own story, translated or

interpreted into fictional terms. Here were the sad boy of
the blacking-factory, the feckless Micawber of a father, the
pretty, shallow Maria, renamed Dora; the young man who
begins his career as a reporter and becomes a famous
author. In Copperfield, he wrote to Forster, he felt he was
sending some part of himself into the Shadowy World.
Most significant of all is the reflection in the 'vague
unhappy loss or want of something'—David's own complaint—of that loss and want in Dickens's life. David
adores the charming Dora, but finds marriage with her a
disappointing emptiness. In time he marries once more—
his second wife is the angelic Agnes Wickfield, a childhood
friend who has been his guiding star. But Agnes is a lifeless
figure, an impossibly good woman with no vigorous
humanity in her. Dickens cannot describe a mature, happy
love-relationship because he does not know it. Kate, the
languorous girl with the heavy-lidded blue eyes, had
become an overweight, sluggish woman, tired with
childbearing, puzzled by her volatile husband, incapable of
real communication with him. 'She is amiable and com-
plying but nothing on earth would make her understand
me.' He had no patience with her pregnancies, treating
them as if they were all her own fault; he mocked her
clumsiness. As a chatelaine he felt she failed him. Kate
undoubtedly felt so too, for her sister Georgina, who had
long ago come to live with the Dickens family, had taken
her place as director of the household, supervisor of the
children, social secretary and companion to Charles. In her
he saw a treasured likeness to the lost Mary: in her he
found the practical qualities and the understanding he
could not get from Kate; yet he was not in love with
Georgina—the vague, unhappy want was still there.

It was not until 1857 that any fulfilment came. He had
founded the journal *Household Words*, had written the rest
of the Christmas Books and *Bleak House*, *Little Dorrit*, and
Hard Times—and had moved to Tavistock House in

Bloomsbury. He had travelled abroad, rejoicing in becoming a cosmopolitan. The youthful, smooth-faced Dickens had vanished, and an impressive figure with a flowing beard had taken his place. He had begun the public readings which were to take him everywhere and increase his fame, as well as giving him an outlet for the dramatic instinct which had always been strong in him, and which had otherwise found expression only in amateur theatricals.

In 1857 he agreed to lend his theatrical experience to the production of a play in Manchester—*The Frozen Deep*, written by Wilkie Collins and himself. Three professional actresses took part in it, a Mrs. Ternan and her two daughters, Maria and Ellen. For Ellen, eighteen years old, he developed an infatuation that was to change his life.

The relationship between Ellen and Dickens remains a mysterious one, despite the probing of biographers and the revelations of recent years. It seems that after a long wooing she capitulated to him with reluctance, and that he led a double life with her at Peckham and elsewhere. There is a story of a child which died in infancy. Georgina and Ellen were friends; when Dickens was dying Ellen was brought to his bedside. The affaire was the well-concealed cause of Dickens's separation from Kate, which came in 1858 and split the Dickens family with divided loyalties. Kate—uncomprehending, ill-used, but uncomplaining—was installed in a house on the edge of Camden Town, with her eldest son, while Dickens and Georgina did their best to cover up the scandal. Dickens does not emerge with conspicuous credit from the unhappy business; though it must be said in his defence that if he did not understand Kate, he did not understand himself either. He was caught up and bemused in middle-aged love, a cataclysmic emotion. It is very likely that he was one of those men who are incapable of love for a woman of their own age, once youth is past, and who ever seek for their own lost youth in girls young enough to be their daughters. It is an unsatisfactory condition, and unhappiness seems to have been the fruit of it for Dickens. We have no written admission of his about Ellen; but she is reflected in three characters, Bella Wilfer of *Our Mutual Friend*, Rosa Bud of *Edwin Drood*, and Estella of *Great Expectations*. It can only have been the knowledge of Ellen that enabled Dickens for the first time to draw portraits of warm, breathing, human girls, not idealized sentimental pictures. Bella and Rosa are temperamental, occasionally difficult—'uncertain, coy and hard to please'. Bella is frankly mercenary, and sharp-tongued into the bargain: Rosa has a rather unromantic passion for eating sweets: Estella is cold-hearted. They are one and the same girl, and such a girl must have brought Dickens torment as well as pleasure. There is no indication in his last novels that the vague unhappy want and loss were ever banished. He must have sought in her the lost angel-spirit Mary, the ideal child, so unlike his own children who were growing up round him and causing him great anxiety. But it nowhere appears that he found the love he needed in Ellen's petulant charm. Even the sure knowledge of that charm has been lost with the years; Ellen looks out from her photograph grave-faced, almost plain, with a high collar and a governess's hair-style.

Lesser men have been inhibited in their careers by emotional difficulties. The genius of Dickens rose above trouble. There is no sign of distraction in the novels of his middle period, though a darkness looms over *Bleak House*, *Little Dorrit* and *Our Mutual Friend* which had not dimmed the earlier books. The stories are dominated by their themes, rather than by their characters: in *Bleak House* the law and its delays, in *Dorrit* the humiliations of the debtors' prison (his old theme) and the emptiness of riches—which he again attacks in *Our Mutual Friend*, together with snobbery and bureaucracy. The London he

loved and hated is a principal actor in these three books.
In *Hard Times* he deserts it for Lancashire, and something
is lost from the book's effect. *A Tale of Two Cities* is the
straightforward historical novel he had attempted in
Barnaby Rudge; but whereas *Barnaby* turned into a rich
Dickensian chronicle, the later book is comparatively stiff,
cold and conventional, with sick humours and a sub-acid
hero. But there are things in these later tales to
replace the animal spirits of *Pickwick* and the Hogarthian
vigour of *Oliver Twist*. From Dickens's mastery of
character come Silas Wegg and Mr. Venus, Young John
Chivery, Mr. Chadband and Mrs. Jellyby, Flora Finching
and Mr. Boffin, the Podsnaps and the Veneerings, Harold
Skimpole—there is no end to the list. The Causes flourish
as ever, as he lashes false charity and all forms of humbug,
and reveals the English scene as he saw it, with anger,
love, and irrepressible humour. If national hypocrisy held
him in artistic chains, as his critic Taine observed, they
could not wholly imprison him.

In *Great Expectations* (1861) he touches maturity. It is
Copperfield over again in its first-person narration and in
its theme of the progress of a puzzled boy. But Pip's story,
unlike David's, is something of an allegory. His life is a
series of lessons learnt the hard way. He finds in Joe
Gargery that simplicity may conceal the highest understanding and wisdom. In the convict Magwitch, brutality
cloaks humble gratitude and generosity. In Estella, he
finds that beauty is a shell when love does not inhabit it.
In the great expectations that bring him riches he finds
disillusion. It is a deeply adult novel, the clue to which may
lie in the character of Estella, Dickens's first completely
cold heroine (for the final hint of hope for Pip's love is a
superimposed happy ending). There is an echo of Ellen
or Nelly in Estella's name, for Dickens could never resist
the temptation to christen his characters associatively.
Disillusion colours *Great Expectations* as Death colours the

last two novels he wrote, *Our Mutual Friend* and *Edwin Drood*, the plot of the first relying upon a body in a river, that of the second upon a body in a vault. At the highest point of his achievement, the shadows were closing upon Dickens.

Ironically enough, it was as his life began its decline that he fulfilled one of his life's ambitions. In his Kentish boyhood, his imagination had been captured by a house called Gad's Hill Place, between Rochester and Gravesend, and he had dreamed of living there. In 1855 he heard that it was available; and in 1860 he sold Tavistock House and made Gad's Hill his permanent family home. Here he spent money and enthusiasm lavishly on making the house of his dreams everything a home could be. From Gad's Hill he again travelled about the country giving those dramatic readings of his own works which fascinated him no less than his audiences, as he became in turn a host of characters, Little Nell, Sergeant Buzfuz, Scrooge, the dying Paul Dombey, and—most electrifying of all—Bill Sikes murdering Nancy. Into these readings he threw all his fiery energies and dramatic abilities, holding audiences by the magic of his voice, as he had previously held them by his writing. People were almost literally hypnotized by the magnetic force of his personality. One who heard him read described the effect: 'He was in himself a whole stock company. He seemed to be physically transformed as he passed from one character to another; he had as many distinct voices as his books had characters; he held at command the fountains of laughter and tears . . . when he sat down it was not mere applause that followed, but a passionate outburst of love for the man.'

In 1867 he took his 'Readings' to America. At first he was apprehensive that the ill-feeling his earlier visit had caused might not have died down. America, however, had forgiven and forgotten, and withheld nothing in the way of welcome and tribute. Everywhere he was enthusiastically received. American hospitality rather exceeded his capacity for it, as he responded to toast after toast of 'Charles Dickens, the guest of the nation'. Poetical greetings were more numerous than on his first visit.

'Come over, then, beloved "Boz", and taste again our wine;
We've forty million grateful hearts, and every one is thine.
Come, at our cordial greeting, come, and tarry with us late;
God bless the ship with prosperous gales, that bears so dear a freight!'

But Dickens was not the young man of 1842, and he could no longer sustain the strain of travel as he had once done. His energy was superhuman, but his body was gradually breaking down. He had not been well in England; in America he was ill, and even the return to England and a quieter life did not cure him. Partial loss of memory, failure of vision, and early symptoms of apoplexy beset him—the result of extreme hurry, overwork, and excitement, his doctor warned him, fourteen months before his death. In spite of this he continued to give the readings, which had become almost compulsive with him. Another American tour tried him to the utmost. On March 15th, 1870, he gave the final reading, and returned to Gad's Hill to work on the book which was to be his last—*Edwin Drood*.

Much has been written of the mystery attached to the ending of the book, which Dickens never lived to write; too little has been said of the quality of the book itself—or of what exists of it. His friend Longfellow, who had read the first monthly parts as they came out in the magazine *All the Year Round*, said when he heard of Dickens's death: 'I hope his book is finished. It is certainly one of his most beautiful works, if not the most beautiful of all.' And so indeed it is. The darkness and disillusion, the biting satire and the confused plot-weaving, are all gone, giving place to a lovely clarity of style. The scene is the Rochester of Dickens's childhood, but a Rochester bathed in an unearthly light, seen through the eyes of a dying man. There are grotesque characters—Durdles and Deputy; satirized characters—Mr. Sapsea and Mrs. Billickin; and an old-style Dickensian lawyer, Mr. Grewgious. Edwin and Rosa, the sweethearts who would not be sweethearts, are real, a pathetic childish pair, and the Cathedral dominates the book. It is ostensibly a story of mystery and murder, of Jasper's dark passions, of revenge and detection; but the atmosphere is one of strange peace. 'Changes of glorious light from moving boughs, songs of birds, scents from gardens, woods and fields . . . penetrate into the Cathedral, subdue its earthly odours, and preach the Resurrection and the Life,' Dickens wrote on the afternoon of June 8th, 1870. On June 9th, he lay dead, struck down by a paralytic seizure. The date was the anniversary of the Staplehurst Railway disaster of 1865, in which he had been involved, and which had haunted him ever since.

The Queen telegraphed her condolences, and the Dean of Westminster agreed with *The Times* that the body of a man so dear to England should lie in Westminster Abbey. They buried him there, in Poets' Corner, instead of in the peaceful Kentish churchyard where he wished to lie; and in Poets' Corner, incongruously surrounded by the bewigged memorials which amused him immensely in life, lies the world's greatest novelist. The febrile, brilliant mind lives on in the characters he created; the friend of the poor and the weak is still fighting for them with words. 'A vast hope has passed across the world,' wrote Alfred de Musset; and Chesterton, many years later, provided an even more telling epitaph:

'Whatever the word "great" means, Dickens was what it means.'